I0118184

Emerging education futures

Experiences and visions from the field

EDITED BY JOHN W. MORAVEC

Education Futures

Contents

Introduction to emerging education futures

JOHN W. MORAVEC

It's tough to make predictions, especially about the future.[1]

We task fewer industries to think about the future like education. In a world awash in accelerating technological and social change, schools today must think about the future and preparing students to be successful in environments and contexts that may differ greatly from what we experience today. But, are we *really* thinking about the future?

Consider the *used future* concept introduced by Sohail Inayatullah:

> *Have you purchased a used future? Is your image of the future, your desired future, yours or is it unconsciously borrowed from someone else? When we look at Asian cities, we see that they tend to follow the same pattern of urban development that western cities did generations ago (Inayatullah, 2004). And yet many, if not most, western mayors now believe that they were mistaken. Instead of spending billions on unplanned growth, development without vision, they should have focused on creating liveable communities. They should have kept green public spaces separating developed regions. They now understand that their image the future—of unbridled growth without concern for nature or livability—led to the gigantic megacities where while many had jobs, they suffered in almost every other way. Asian cities have unconsciously followed this pattern. They have forgotten their own traditions where village life and community were central, where living with nature was important. Now they must [find] ways to create new futures, or continue to go along with the future being discarded elsewhere. This used future is leading to a global crisis of fresh water depletion [and] climate change, not to mention human dignity. (Inayatullah, 2008, p. 5)*

---

1   Variations of this quote are attributed to many sources, including Neils Bohr, Mark Twain, Sam Goldwyn, and Yogi Berra.

Education and schooling are prime examples of used futures that lead to a crisis of relevance, following the same patterns of top-down pedagogies, age separation, absence of play, etc. We designed our systems to meet certain goals centuries ago, yet we continue to fool ourselves into thinking we are changing the paradigm by introducing new technologies and social situations when, in reality, we are simply remixing the same formula.

It is for this reason that it is challenging to imagine a future for education that differs greatly from what we have employed in the past. I argue, we have a crisis of imagination in education and schooling. 'Schools' depicted in popular science fiction shows such as *Star Trek*, *Starship Troopers*, and even *Ender's Game* would be immediately recognizable as a school to any person who lived 100 years ago. The concept of what a school is and does seems immutable despite huge shifts in the needs of society and advancements in technology. If we are to educate effectively for the future, it is especially important to expand our thinking to confront ideas or assumptions about teaching and learning that hold us in the past.

This volume presents a compendium of diverse experiences and ideas to help spark new thinking among educators and policymakers. We aim to provoke conversation and facilitate new ideas for meeting human capital development needs in rapidly transforming societies. With authors spanning four continents, this book reveals a 'snapshot' of our best thinking for building new education futures. Chapters focus variously on primary through tertiary-level education, as well as looking at the idea of 'education' more broadly.

It is always interesting to learn what 'others' are thinking or doing and to expand our thinking a bit. The authors in this book provide diverse perspectives across cultures, and I do not expect readers to agree with all ideas presented. What this book contains, however, are ideas and practices from a competitive call for submissions that each author believes is helping to push the future of education across diverse contexts. While all chapters underwent an editing process, I strived to ensure the 'voice' of each author remained true to themselves.

I divided this book into two parts. The first part focuses on experiences and research from the field. The second part presents visions and ideas for the future of education.

Leona Ungerer looks at how artificial intelligence impacts higher education. She briefly introduces the field of AI, discussing many opportunities that the mode of technology offers. And, she also addresses concerns about incorporating it in higher education contexts, especially in emerging countries such as South Africa, where an ecosystem is forming to support applications of AI in education.

Focusing on competency-based education, **Lisa Bosman**, **Julius Keller**, and **Gary Bertoline** share experiences from Perdue University's new B.S. in Transdisciplinary Studies in Technology. In their program, they require students to show master in 20 core competencies. Transdisciplinarity is enabled by integrating humanities with engineering, design, and technology skill sets, together with providing students agency to individualize one-third of their learning experience through classes and learning experiences of their choosing.

Audrey Falk and **Russell Olwell** take us on a journey, relating their experiences building the Community Engagement Institute at Merrimack College in Massachusetts with an eye toward enabling transformational learning and social justice in the campus and the local community. In moving toward interdisciplinary approaches, they discuss breaking down departmental and discipline 'silos' that compartmentalize higher education, share their experiences in building partnerships and other relationships with their community, and building a culture of inclusivity and transparency through student engagement.

Since 2012, **Silvia Cecila Enríquez** has organized a virtual community of practice (CoP) called *Docentes en línea* at the National University of La Plata in Argentina. In her chapter co-authored with **Sandra Gargiulo**, **Jimena Ponz**, and **Erica Scorians**, they connect their work in developing a CoP for online educators with the principles of *Manifesto 15*. In their experience in curating a diverse community of co-creators, they believe teachers cannot become agents of change unless if *they change themselves* as learners.

Writing from Bratislava, Slovakia, **Robert Thorn** shares his exploration of working with the question, what do young people really need from education? He sets out to look at happiness and success made through the decisions by young people he and his school has taught and suggests a different approach with different goals should be adopted: a *learner-development-centered* approach. This holistic approach, he believes, helps to build trust, provide youth with a reason for attending school, reframes roles for teachers, and allows pathways for parents to guide their children toward wisdom to a greater extent.

Erling Dahl, **Einar Strømmen**, and **Tor Syvertsen** provide an overview of what they consider a quiet, guerrilla action at the Norwegian University of Science and Technology in Trondheim: breaking from the use of traditional textbooks and eliminating lectures and formal exams. In their doctoral-level course, *Rheology and non-Newtonian fluids*, they developed an approach based on heutagogical principles. They found that students could break beyond the academic confines of a typical graduate course and built compendia that made the course content more relevant for their personal lines of research and professional activity.

The second part of the book departs from experiences and focuses on visions and ideas, providing space for creativity and inspiration to emerge. **Kelly Killorn** and I attempted to break free from used futures thinking, opening with a provocative question: *Does the future need schools?* In a small study involving an expert panel of respondents, we sought to build insight into what and why we are educating. Our investigation revealed an intriguing ecology of ideas that showed, yes, we can think about schools differently.

Pekka Ihanainen, a Finnish teacher educator, is one of the most abstract, conceptual thinkers I have ever known. He is a crafter of ideas. He shows this in his professional work, but also in art, be it painting or igniting a fire sculpture at his cabin home, blending modernity with traditionalism. His canvas in this book presents a rich palette of pedagogical *affordances*—objects, places, and events that make it possible to do something in teaching and learning. The ideas he presents calls for a new mindset in education that take into consideration complex interactions between affordances of *observability*, *solvability*, and *partakeability*.

We left lots of room on the top of these pages

Stefania Savva from the Cyprus University of Technology provides a framework of thought, called *multiliteracies dynamic affinity spaces* (MDAS). Writing as a response to Cristóbal Cobo's chapter in *Knowmad Society* on skills and competencies for knowmadic workers (2013), she draws conclusions from her doctoral research, investigating the nature of multimodal, digitally mediated literacies and their implementation in an informal learning context. She suggests students' repertoires of literacy are empowered as they engage in the learning process as active designers and multimodal learners.

Focusing on teacher training, **Gabriela Carreño Murillo**, a trainer and researcher at the Normal School of Atizapán de Zaragoza in Mexico, provides four 21st century teacher profiles: the knowmad, the divergent, the craftsman, and reflexive. Teacher training, she argues, needs to move away from a formal exercise into something that better recognizes the humanness of the professional development experience, integrating lifelong, informal, non-formal, and serendipitous elements of learning.

As a compendium of diverse ideas, not all of Part II of this volume is scientific. **Erik Miletić** presents a *Reason-Emotion-Instinct* (REI) model for education that is built on the writing by the late Slovenian marketing guru, Igor Kenda ("Eros," 2012). This chapter was selected for inclusion as a thought piece—Kenda's writing sparked something in Miletić, who in turn writes that we should consider educating for the development of the three intellects and appreciate students where they are on each. It provides a perspective, together with a suggested framework, for rethinking education to better connect with the human experience.

Finally, while working on edits to this volume, my niece, **Zoe Moravec**, approached me and asked, "what are you working on, Uncle?" I told her that this book is about the future of schools and learning, and she drew a picture and shared what she thought the school of the future would look like (included in the visual introduction to Part II on pp. 140-141). It looks similar to what we have today. Students sit in rows, but they sit closer together in a smaller classroom with a large screen in front. And, the teacher is seated in a cubicle in the back of the room. I asked, "so what is different?" She struggled for words but emphasized the classroom has a *heart* and that we would find what's different in the heart.

for you to write your own notes, doodle, & play!

It is what you take with you from year to year, she explained. The teacher, the other students, and what you learn are the heart, and it always stays with you and changes you.

Perhaps this, too, is an illustration of a used future. It is difficult to find words to describe anything different in education. I believe we each have at least bits and pieces of what an alternate future for education could look like, but we often struggle to find the right words. That's why it is so important to share our ideas and visions. Even if they sometimes make little sense to broader audiences, at least we are progressing toward creating new meanings.

If the vision of where we want to be in the future is not crystal clear, it is beneficial to start with a vision and principles for how we would like to get there. On January 1, 2015, we released *Manifesto 15*, a statement of principles for building new futures in education. As the lead writer, I intended the document to set an inspiring vision to challenges the norm—but it also presents a vision backed by research and experience. As several authors reference the manifesto in this volume, the full text is included as an appendix.

This is a book of experiences, visions, and ideas. Again, you are not expected to accept every idea presented. I believe that if an idea makes me think and pushes me to learn more, it's worth discussing. This book is designed to challenge and inspire our thinking. Read it critically and make it your own. The same invitation applies as in our earlier work, *Knowmad Society*:

> *If you are holding onto a paper copy of this book, please do not treat it like a book. Write on it, draw on the margins, highlight the parts you like, and write "bullshit" over the parts you do not like. Tear out pages; mix in your own ideas, and share alike with others. This entire volume is Creative Commons licensed, which means that we encourage you to copy, redistribute, and remix this work. All that we ask is that you share it alike with others, give proper credit for the ideas you use, and let us know how you have added to the conversation. (Moravec, 2013, p. 25)*

Just as the future is yet to be written, this is a book that does not pretend to have all the best answers and needs your extra love and attention to grow even more. Make it your own. Write and draw on it, highlight the parts you like, and tear out what you don't like. Customize it and build it into your own guide to building new futures for education. And, please share alike with us and others so we may learn from you.

John W. Moravec
Minneapolis, Minnesota
john@educationfutures.com

REFERENCES

Cobo, C. (2013). Skills and competencies for knowmadic workers. In Moravec, J.W. (Ed.), *Knowmad Society* (pp. 57-88). Minneapolis: Education Futures.

"Eros". (2012). *[psi]*. Maribor, Slovenia: DCC Marketing.

Inayatullah, S. (2004). Cities create their future. *Journal of Futures Studies, 8*(3), 77-81.

Inayatullah, S. (2008). Six pillars: futures thinking for transforming. *Foresight, 10*(1), 4-21. doi: 10.1108/14636680810855991

Moravec, J.W. (Ed.). (2013). *Knowmad Society*. Minneapolis: Education Futures.

Moravec, J.W. et al. (2015). *Manifesto 15*. Minneapolis: Education Futures. manifesto15.org

Notes

notes

Part I

Experiences

7X10=70

7X6=42

7X

1

7X8=56

7X2=14

=28   7X7=49   7X2=1

7X5=35   7X1=7

AI in higher education: Considering the ecosystem in an emerging-country context

LEONA UNGERER

If universities do not adopt the new scientific agenda for research and learning resulting from artificial intelligence (AI), they will gradually lose their relevance, culminating in redundancy (Gann & Dodgson, 2017). Rometty (as cited in Raymone, 2018) further predicts that AI will impact 100% of jobs, professions, and industries. Time will tell the extent to which these predictions will come true, but in the short term, AI's relentless growth compels people to change the way they work (Bragg, 2018).

The intense contemporary technological transformations experienced globally cannot merely be ascribed to the third industrial revolution, but rather herald the outset of a fourth industrial revolution in which a blend of technologies blurs the distinction between the physical, digital, and biological spheres (Schwab, 2016). Developments in fields such as AI, robotics, genetics, nanotechnology, 3D printing, and biotechnology augment and intensify existing trends (World Economic Forum, 2016).

The impact of the above intense global technological revolution, including AI's exceptional growth, is also felt on the African continent (Abardazzou, 2017). AI may offer considerable opportunities for emerging countries if approached in an open-minded manner, focusing on the possibilities that it offers. Emerging countries should, however, also consider existing concerns in the field such as bias in its applications. Ideally, emerging countries should be involved in developing new technological systems from their outset (Harman, as cited in *Business Tech*, 2018). By delivering diverse researchers in the field of AI, emerging countries could play a key role in eradicating some existing biases, feature in developing technological systems from their outset and employ this technology for the greater good of their communities. If AI is used for the greater good of humanity, it will offer significantly more advantages than threats (Tegmark, 2017). Ethical guidelines should underlie the implementation of AI throughout.

Similar to previous *techno-political* revolutions, various groups' experiences with AI will mainly depend on human decisions taken in the field of AI (Letouzé & Pentland, 2018). Africa's known strengths, such as ample, affordable labour and its natural resources, seem not to meet the requirements of the fourth industrial revolution, which include massive investment capital, research and development, and highly skilled human capital. However, if properly managed, the present industrial revolution may offer an opportunity for Africa to become

an important role-player in the global economy (Abardazzou, 2017). A report
by the McKinsey Global Institute (as cited in Adepoju, 2017) predicts that by
2025, automation will replace between 45 and 75 million jobs globally, jobs
that are filled by more than half of Africa's current workers. However, Africa
may potentially leap-frog some earlier technological developments if it acts
swiftly and develop its human capital. This type of rapid, non-linear progress
already took place in a number of sectors on the African continent, including the
banking and telecommunications sector. Many African countries, for instance,
bypassed the phase of systematically installing phone lines, by rather relying
on cell phone services for communication (Winthrop, 2016). They increased the
pace of innovation by directly adopting advanced technology, instead of first
employing customary, less effective technologies (Brooks, 2019).

Africa should urgently equip its youth with the required skills to contribute
to the development of AI through research and innovation (Abardazzou, 2017).
A focus on STEM skills would be essential, and the education system should
enhance innovation and entrepreneurship. China and India may serve as role-
models for African countries in this regard because they have overcome many
challenges that are also experienced on the African continent. For instance,
they did not actively participate in the first and second industrial revolutions,
but by developing their human capital, they have become part of the fastest-
growing economies in the world and contribute significantly to technological
advancement (Adepoju, 2017). Lee (2017) warns that those countries that do
not feature among the leaders in AI may be compelled to collaborate with the
leading country supplying most of their AI software and become economically
dependent on it. Dependent countries may accept investments from the leading
AI country, while its AI companies benefit from the dependent country's users,
signifying possible neo-colonialism, described as the "geopolitical practice of
using capitalism, business globalization, and imperialism to control society
instead of either direct military control or indirect political control" (Gbara,
2008, p. 107).

Since the future work context makes new demands on human beings such
as being able to work effectively alongside machines, focusing on their uniquely

human traits that the most sophisticated robots cannot imitate, they should reconsider their demands on education, particularly higher education (Aoun, 2018). Suitably preparing students for the digital age involves an awareness of both the capabilities and limitations of technology, while "robot-proof education" develops human beings' unique capabilities such as creativity and collaboration. Auon (2018) introduces a new discipline, *humanics*, aimed at promoting uniquely human traits such as creativity and flexibility. It builds on inherent human strengths and prepares students for a labour force where human professionals work along with intelligent machines.

Views about artificial intelligence

There is no consensus yet about the definition of AI. However, AI broadly relates to the capacity of machines and systems to gain and apply knowledge and perform intelligent behaviour (OECD, 2018). AI tools are capable of carrying out various cognitive tasks, including sensing, processing spoken language and making decisions, and then undertaking additional tasks such as moving and manipulating objects based on the outcomes of the cognitive tasks. A blend of processes such as big data analytics, cloud computing, machine-to-machine communication and the Internet of Things (IoT) guide the operation and learning processes of intelligent systems (ESCAP, 2017).

As software, AI is typically guided by algorithms, but physical entities, such as robots, are necessary to reflect its functions (e.g. talking) that resemble the functioning of a human brain. AI advancement has mainly taken place in domains such as large-scale machine learning, deep learning, natural language processing (NLP), collaborative systems, computer vision, algorithmic game theory, and computational social choice and soft robotics (ESCAP, 2017).

According to Makhdoomi (2018), the form of AI that is mostly used at the moment is *narrow AI*, performing minor tasks, for instance, facial recognition software and Apple's Siri. Makhdoomi (2018) foresees challenges when *general AI*, superior to humans on all tasks involving human cognition, becomes established. Tegmark (2017) posits that computer intelligence may ultimately equal or exceed human intelligence, a perspective known as *strong AI*. Supporters of the weak AI perspective believe that computer intelligence will not be able to exceed human intelligence, mainly because of differences between the two types of intelligence. Computers further adhere to code and do not have the free will not to do so, unless programmed otherwise. Finally, it is challenging to develop computer programmes that truly show human qualities such as abstract thinking, emotions, and intuition (Tegmark, 2017).

Possible uses of AI in education

Universities will soon feel the impact of AI, considering the developments and investments in this field (Popenici & Kerr, 2017). Adams Becker, Brown, Dahlstrom, Davis, DePaul, Diaz, and Pomerant (2018) project that AI may be adopted (but they did not indicate to what extent) in the field of higher education by 2021. The market for AI technologies in the education sector is expected to grow by about 50 percent by 2022 (Technavio, as cited in Adams Becker et al., 2018). Trends driving higher education institutions to investigate AI solutions include increasing student numbers resulting from the democratisation and internationalisation of higher education (Popenici & Kerr, 2017).

AI will disrupt higher education, especially because it already features in basic tasks such as grading, data analysis and statistical analysis in a higher education context (Lynch, 2018). AI may assist *inter alia* in augmenting online learning, enriching adaptive learning software and sustaining research processes because of its ability to interact intuitively with students. According to Popenici and Kerr (2017), *teacherbots* are already replacing teaching assistants to some extent by being assigned administrative teaching tasks such as delivering content and providing administrative feedback. By letting AI take care of routine tasks, teaching staff's time could be freed up to focus on essential tasks, including research (Adams Becker et al., 2018).

By applying available data and algorithms, AI and machine learning may assist educators in predicting individual students' learning rate, their levels of comprehension and progress, and the challenges posed by particular content and learning approaches. It is possible to customise an interactive learning path for each student based on their learning requirements by taking into account their courses, online interactions, and scores on assessments (Choudhury, 2018). Universities such as Georgia State University and Arizona State

University use AI to track individual students' performance, predict their marks and suggest interventions when necessary. The application of data analytics in cases involving students and staff raises serious concerns about privacy and confidentiality. Solid codes of practice are required for guiding decisions in this field (Gann & Dodgson, 2017). In this regard, Drabwell (2018) warns that the ethical consequences of AI in education (AIED) tools, such as personalised learning systems, are rarely considered and that guidelines are required to guide decisions about ethical issues resulting from the use of AI in education.

AI can reduce teachers' load when assigned cumbersome tasks such as tutoring, grading and providing feedback. It changes the learning environment through the creation of virtual assistants who are able to think, act, interact, and supply customised content and personalized care. Students often feel more comfortable about learning through trial and error when interacting with a robot rather than a human, because they may fear losing face when providing incorrect answers (Choudhury, 2018).

Educators globally further need to be cognisant of the revolution in AI and its implications for education (Shivhare, 2019). They should be equipped to use AI for the greater good of society (Seldon & Abedoye, 2018). AI may offer a completely new way of providing high-quality education globally, especially to the masses that do not yet have access to it (Seldon & Abedoye, 2018). Choudhury (2018) regards AI as the biggest accelerator for the modernisation of education. Although the educational AI revolution may still be in its initial stages, it has already generated innovative approaches that have improved teachers' and students' efficiency and lowered the costs of the public-school system.

UNESCO (as cited in Choudhury, 2018) estimates that 68.8 million teachers will be needed globally by 2030 to keep class sizes below 40 students at the secondary school level. It would be difficult to find and train such a large number of teachers during the next ten years as many countries do not have the necessary infrastructure for addressing these needs. The use of AI could alleviate this situation because it facilitates education, making it accessible to more people (Maskey, 2018). Automated grading programmes could free up educators' time, allowing them more time to interact with students. Some of these programmes are already piloted in countries such as India and China to determine their efficiency in an emerging country context. In terms of student efficiency, AI systems such as Apple's Siri and Google's adaptive learning algorithm programme empower students to gather information in completely new ways (Choudhury, 2018).

AI essentially will make educators' lives easier (Choudhury, 2018). Considering its potential, African governments should focus on establishing working groups to investigate possible applications of AI in an education context to guide the development and implementation of suitable AI tools and techniques. This type of collaboration will support the standardisation of AI applications in an education context and prevent possible duplication (University of Pretoria, 2018).

Why artificial intelligence will not replace expert human educators

Educators will have to justify their existence increasingly during the next two decades considering increased demands that teaching should become automated and "teacher-proof" (Selwyn, 2018). Expert human educators offer six benefits that may be disregarded when the focus is on automating teaching. Human educators have gained their knowledge by learning themselves; they establish both cognitive and social connections with students; they use natural speech; they use their bodies during communication; and, they are able to improvise (Selwyn, 2018).

During teaching, students benefit both from educators' knowledge and their recollections of how they have gained their knowledge. Although the required learning content can be uploaded onto technology, AI is not capable of learning something in the same way as humans do and then transferring this learning to other humans (Selwyn, 2018). Educators are able to approach matters from their students' perspective and to establish cognitive connections with students during their learning attempts. Although computer science has advanced considerably, machines are not yet able to detect and model this type of thinking. Teaching further requires involvement from both educators and students because educators would not be able to bring about learning if students did not cooperate. Educators often focus on encouraging student engagement and motivating their students, which require interpersonal skills that machines do not have. Educators typically do not adhere to a pre-set text when they teach; they adapt the information that they present based on students' reactions, while students learn to listen for relevant content during this process (Selwyn, 2018). Educators often serve as a source of inspiration for students, encouraging them to think for themselves and come up with new ideas, something that AI is not capable of (Harper, 2018). AI further is unable to guide students in developing social and emotional learning skills that take place during human teaching interactions (Poth, 2018).

Human educators use their bodies as a resource when they teach. Their movements, intonation, and register (e.g. when they lower their voices) convey subtle messages. Humans also typically respond completely differently to the presence of another person than to the most human-like simulation (Selwyn, 2018). Finally, the human capability for improvising plays an essential role in effective teaching. Although planning beforehand, educators are able to adapt to circumstances in the classroom. Effective teaching often involves creativity, spontaneity, and innovativeness, attributes that computer systems typically do not reflect (Selwyn, 2018).

Empathy fulfils a vital role in the learning process, an attribute that AI does not embody. Some main challenges of contextualising AI to real-world scenarios involve teaching computers the ability to take in a particular context and being able to act intuitively (Lambert, 2018). As is evident above, expert human educators offer capabilities for supporting learning that technology cannot imitate perfectly (Selwyn, 2018). There currently seems to be very little risk that AI will take over skilled educators' jobs or outperform them. Concerns about possible risks resemble experiences in other industries where the impact of AI generates anxiety, mainly because of misconceptions about the technology. Properly introducing educators to AI and guiding them to use AI tools effectively should alleviate their existing concerns (Loeffner, 2018). In a higher education context, an important initial step would be to incorporate AI techniques such as machine learning in the professional development of academic staff (Adams Becker et al., 2018).

The ecosystem in an emerging-country context

It appears that AI holds considerable promise for higher education as it supports modern types of pedagogy, for instance, by being oriented toward the support of personalised learning. However, the characteristics of the broader ecosystem will impact on the diffusion of an innovation such as AI, because conditions in an emerging-country context differ vastly from those in the developed world.

It has been suggested that South Africa, an emerging country, should develop the necessary competencies to participate efficiently in a future AI-rich environment. However, some structural limitations may restrict the successful incorporation of new technologies into the country's economy. For example, there are concerns about the quality of education systems and scientific research institutions, and there are concerns about insufficient infrastructure for sustaining growth. Fostering AI success, for instance, to ensure the country's global competitiveness, requires vibrant ecosystems supported by five pillars, namely universities, start-ups, large companies, policymakers and multi-stakeholder partnerships (EE Publishers, 2017).

AI holds many opportunities and challenges for emerging countries. Its opportunities include increasing emerging countries' national competitiveness and supporting the delivery of the sustainable development goals, while some challenges include ethical risks, a "new frontier technology divide" and technological unemployment (ESCAP, 2017). AI appears to have potential applications in all sectors and industries, and may potentially contribute to attaining all sustainable development goals (ESCAP, 2017). The implementation of AI holds considerable promise, especially in humanitarian areas, which may be particularly relevant for emerging countries with their limited resources. By unleashing the power of AI, stakeholders such as non-governmental organizations (NGOs) and governments may be able to improve the quality of life of local communities (Maskey, 2018). AI has initially only been applied on a limited scale in emerging countries to resolve particular problems in a specified area. It would, however, be possible to address more complex issues as machine learning progresses and AI is used more widely. If properly adopted, AI may enhance people's daily lives in areas such as education and health care and may play a role in addressing issues related to poverty and malnutrition. It, therefore, is essential that NGOs and governments in developing countries leverage AI's true potential (Maskey, 2018).

Ensuring inclusive and equitable quality education and promoting lifelong learning opportunities for all, a Sustainable Development Goal, is a particular challenge in emerging countries (ESCAP, 2017). Developing countries often lack the experienced teachers and resources required to sustain proper teaching. Many students in rural areas walk long distances to school, which contributes to poor school attendance and education gaps. In terms of contributing to high-quality education, AI tools such as personal learning assistants may assist in making tutoring services and learning materials accessible to students in these conditions (Maskey, 2018). Maharaj (as cited in Gower, 2018) comments on how AI could contribute to achieving social justice in South Africa and advises that building sustainable services in South Africa's rural regions would require vision and investment. To address the shortage of good mathematics and science teachers in rural areas, teachers in urban areas could hologram themselves into classrooms in rural areas through future telecommunications technology, such as fifth-generation technology, allowing learners to interact with them in real-time. It should also soon be possible to automate machines that would enable students to learn basic concepts without a tutor, learning any time they want, wherever they are. Stakeholders in the field of AI should be cognisant of the strengths and concerns of emerging countries, as well as AI's restrictions, to generate locally relevant applications (Maskey, 2018).

Pedroncelli (2018) describes the revolutionary impact that AI technology had in some African industries. In an education context, M-Shule, a Kenyan start-up, provides personalised education to primary school students in various African countries through using AI and text messaging. In a programme known as the AI Family Challenge, I-Innovate, a South African educational technology company, introduces students and their families to AI, enabling them to explore AI technologies such as speech recognition, machine learning, and autonomous vehicles. In an education-related field, a South Africa-based AI-enabled recruitment platform, Leaply, enables companies to screen graduates in a cost-effective, efficient manner. Leaply currently operates in 15 African countries.

Governments in emerging countries have a key role to play in ethical and governance considerations. Balancing people's privacy and the openness of data presents a further ethical dilemma, and achieving a suitable balance between privacy, ownership, and transparency may be particularly challenging (ESCAP, 2017). Watters (2017) further warns that AI is not simply a technological development, but may also perpetuate ideology, because it is not developed in isolation. The idea that AI supports personalisation may be highly valued in contexts where individualism and consumption are of the essence. However, considering a general lack of insight into how the algorithms guiding AI arrive at decisions, it is not clear what personalizsation truly involves. Those who are at the receiving end of these decisions may not know how the decisions were made and whether any recourse is available to them, signifying possible oppression.

AI may reproduce established beliefs and practices, and often reflects existing societal biases (Bragg, 2018). AI algorithms may perpetuate the contexts and biases inherent in the environments where they were created; an example of this is the trend that certain voice recognition software does not recognise particular accents. AI algorithms often are created in developed countries and may consequently not be sufficiently sensitive to the contexts of developing countries (Harman, as cited in *Business Tech*, 2018; Marwala, 2018). Avedisian and Matsumoto (2018) advise that AI tools do not sufficiently reflect diverse voices and cultural data, and overlook the experiences of large constituents of the global population. Marwala (2018), an established scientist in the field of AI, relates his experiences with AI where voice recognition software has been unable to identify his accent. He recommends a new form of activism in the South African economic and educational contexts to address bias and discrimination in technology, such as recording and archiving South African accents and selling the resulting data to companies that create voice recognition devices. "AI needs to be revolutionized and deracialized—and this requires research and interventions from scholars and scientists, a new activism, that goes beyond the creation of new algorithms" (Marwala, as cited in

Butler-Adam, 2018, p. 1). AI models may deliver biased results when for instance, a population, does not feature strongly in the data used to train the particular model (Cheatham, Javanmardian & Samandari, 2019). Scientists from diverse demographic backgrounds would especially contribute to addressing the this imbalance (Marwala, 2018).

Nearly four decades ago, Toffler (as cited in Gillies, 2017) predicted a future where everyone would become involved in the production process while at the same time consuming, becoming what he termed 'prosumers.' Technology would be the mechanism empowering people to produce the objects that they consume. By contributing to and taking a lead in the development of appropriate AI solutions for emerging country contexts, people in these regions would be able to create their own solutions, becoming prosumers of AI and not having to look to technology producers for possible solutions.

Although many people globally benefit from the Internet such a being able to share information with large numbers of users, billions still do not. Information communication technology (ICT) infrastructure is essential for introducing AI, which may create a new frontier technology divide. Broadband infrastructure is an essential requirement for the extensive deployment of AI; developed countries that often have vast high-speed broadband networks can invest in AI, while emerging countries are unable to participate to the same extent (ESCAP, 2017). For citizens and business on the African continent to benefit fully from AI, broadband coverage will have to be significantly increased, especially in rural areas (University of Pretoria, 2018).

Although technological unemployment is a potential concern relating to the impact of AI, it certainly is not a given. Automation or robots do not necessarily equate to AI, therefore AI does not necessarily play a role in all job losses ascribed to automation or robotics (ESCAP, 2017). The fear of new technologies replacing workers is nothing new. What has changed, however, is that newer technologies such as AI offer more comprehensive capabilities than previous types of technology (*Business Tech*, 2018). This does not only contribute to jobs being replaced but also to the disruption and restructuring of industries as a whole. Because of a lack of efficient education systems and skills, it may be difficult for people in a country such as South Africa to be retrained for the envisaged new technology-intensive jobs. Governments, especially those of developing countries, grapple with the question of how to prepare for the implications of new technologies and the required new business models (*Business Tech*, 2018).

Harman (as cited in *Business Tech*, 2018) adds an increased concentration of wealth to the above concerns. He suggests that wealthy people would adopt AI and other technologies more readily than those less well-off, providing them an unfair advantage in terms of their productive capacity. New technologies may further lead to new business models that would make it possible to control many subsectors of an industry, thereby limiting competition. The onus would be on governments to keep up with developments in the field of AI and to deal effectively with them, for example by addressing concerns about intellectual property and competition law. Many developing country governments, however, do not pay sufficient attention to these matters (Harman, as cited in *Business Tech*, 2018).

Creating a vibrant AI ecosystem in South Africa

South Africa must create a vibrant ecosystem that allows the power of AI to be unleashed. As has been suggested above, the country needs a complete, extended vision of the deployment of AI in its economy, with a focus on responsible AI. The challenges that South Africa faces in adopting AI may not differ considerably from those faced by other countries and include preparing stakeholders for the issues to be considered when AI is gradually adopted in all spheres of life, including the technological, political, ethical and social spheres. Businesses are responsible for preparing their workforces for the changes resulting from AI. For example, workers should be trained to work with newly developed machines (EE Publishers, 2017).

AI will obviously generate new jobs and the need for new skills, for instance in areas such as robotics. Some jobs may become redundant and inequality may be worsened. Therefore, it is essential that policymakers prepare for possible challenges resulting from the adoption of AI and identify groups at risk of losing their jobs. They should develop strategies to prepare groups that are at risk to be re-integrated into the economy (EE Publishers, 2017).

Preparing for the impact of AI requires more than merely focusing on jobs. Rules and regulations also have to be formulated. For example: Who would be responsible for deciding about the codes of ethics that would guide algorithms? AI generates both opportunities and responsibilities for stakeholders such as business and government. These stakeholders should ensure that the elements required for the successful implementation of AI are in place. These include suitable governance models, ethical, privacy, and security guidelines that generate trust and a solid code of conduct. South Africa's success in implementing AI depends on the following, among others: reconsidering the human-machine relationship; revising business models and processes; and, creating a flourishing ecosystem, as discussed above (EE Publishers, 2017).

Stakeholders and policymakers at local, national and international levels should ensure the protection of basic human capabilities and goals during the development and use of AI (University of Montreal, 2018). Various issues need to be considered, including empowering citizens who have to adapt to the changes resulting from digital technologies with educational opportunities that support critical thinking, respect, and accountability, preparing them to participate appropriately in a sustainable digital society. Considering the importance of ethics in the deployment of AI, a solid ethical framework should underlie decisions about implementing appropriately implementing AI in an emerging-country context.

The role of educational institutions in preparing the future workforce

The future work environment will involve completely new, advanced technologies, with AI driving automation to increase productivity through fewer sources (Chatlani, 2018). Employers and education stakeholders, realising the inevitability of these trends, are concerned about suitably preparing students for the future workforce (Chatlani, 2018). A change in skills is not all that is necessary. According to a recent Universities UK report (as cited in *The Guardian*, 2018), educational delivery approaches may have to be completely reconsidered and the linear model of receiving education, entering employment and pursuing a career may not suffice anymore. The focus should be on flexible partnerships between universities and employers, and new course layouts.

Oblinger (2018) points out that AI and robotics, as fields of study, require new majors and certificate programmes at higher education institutions. Albelli (2018) further foresees that a large part of the workforce will soon need qualifications in areas such as data science, cloud computing, and mobile and software development. The number of graduates with STEM degrees at educational institutions should be increased and technical skills deserve more attention in K-12 education. She suggests that students could be required to study a computer science language such as Python in addition to or instead of mastering a foreign language, as is often required. However, considering that a specific computer language may be extinct by the time some students graduate, a focus on computational thinking may rather be advisable. It is increasingly recognised in education systems globally that computational problem-solving (being able to think logically and in an algorithmic manner, and creating artefacts such as models utilising computational tools) is a required competency in most fields. Computational thinking, as an essential skill, could even be added as the "5th C" of 21st century skills to the existing four skills (critical thinking, creativity, collaboration and communication) that should inform school curricula (Grover, 2018).

The AI revolution is irreversible (Makhdoomi, 2018) and AI will certainly affect students' careers (Glass, 2018). Students interested in careers in AI may choose from a range of fields such as data science, advanced statistics, and machine learning. Students who are not necessarily interested in a career in AI should also benefit from an introduction to the basics of AI and working with machines.

The complexities involved in people's work and in having to work with progressively competent machines should be considered. The real challenge for higher education institutions is not to focus on how education is delivered, but on how phenomena such as AI, analytics, robotics and the required extensive collaboration impact on the substance of education. The content of what students learn, the meaning of higher education credentials and the methods for keeping up with change may need to change (Oblinger, 2018).

Technical skills such as coding, data science design thinking and the ability to interact suitably with technologies such as AI and machine learning are gaining importance in the current work environment (Albelli, 2018). *Soft skills* such as proper interpersonal communication, curiosity, creativity, empathy, and critical thinking complement these technical skills. The essence of suitable soft skills is evident in the terms used to describe them, such as power skills (Bragg, 2018), employability skills (Gonser, 2018) and metacognitive skills (Aoun, 2018). Employees in a current work environment also have to collaborate efficiently. As mentioned by Oblinger (2018), employees seeing that teams with a common purpose support innovation.

By placing a stronger emphasis on critical thinking, synthesising and analysing data and problem-solving in higher education curricula, higher education institutions may prepare students for demonstrating the vital hard skills required in the current workplace. Merely memorising and reciting facts is not sufficient anymore. Higher education institutions could better align their curricula to industry needs through enhanced collaboration with businesses (Albelli, 2018). Suitable business-education partnerships would support student-directed learning, blending traditional education and workplace knowledge, developing their problem-solving skills based on real-world understanding. When students gain first-hand experience of the business problems companies experience, it would ignite their interest in learning how to solve those problems (McBride, as cited in Lachs, 2017). Suitable business-education partnerships would also assist students in understanding their role as team members, preparing them for successful collaboration (Caplan, 2018).

It is evident that educational institutions may prepare students for their role in the future workforce by integrating more soft skills in their curricula. Employees may increasingly be required to do non-routine work and therefore need higher-level cognitive skills such as critical thinking, data literacy, problem-solving skills, creativity and the ability to collaborate in real time. Considering the importance of mission-driven teams in the work environment, educational institutions especially need to incorporate teamwork and collaborative learning in curricula. Education systems typically support individual success and may not prepare students for the high-level collaboration necessary for innovation. Providing students with more team-based assignments and considering their ability to collaborate efficiently with others during evaluation may alleviate this situation (Albelli, 2018). In a knowledge society where information is easily accessible, the focus in learning is not on extracting knowledge, but on building it (Harper, 2018).

Considering that a curious mind-set and openness to new learning will be essential requirements for future workers, educational institutions should encourage growth mind-sets and cognitive flexibility among students. Students' future employability may depend on how well they can adapt, learn new material and apply their learning to new situations (Albeli, 2018). Technologies such as virtual reality and AI may serve well to immerse students in real-world experiences, make their learning personalised and enhance their engagement during this process (Lachs, 2017). Further requirements preparing them for the future world of work would be students' willingness to learn continuously, their resilience and their adaptability (Albeli, 2018).

Humans cannot compete with AI in terms of efficiency, accuracy, knowledge and incessant replication. Irrespective of the subject they teach, educators should instil important human capabilities such as creative problem-solving, inventiveness, collaboration, leadership, empathy and resilience in their students. Focusing on human attributes that distinguish them from machines is important in preparing them for the future (Makhdoomi, 2018).

According to Glass (2018), universities can prepare students by adapting their curricula, collaborating with business and providing mentorship programmes. It may be challenging for universities to keep abreast of all changes in the technology industry, but they should investigate their core curricula to ensure that they prepare students for the future workforce. Essential fields to include are computer science, entrepreneurship and social impact studies. Computer science should provide students with an understanding of the back-end systems that drive machines, and entrepreneurship would prepare students for the continuous innovation required across industries (Glass, 2018). Marishane (as cited in Buthelezi, 2017) emphasises that entrepreneurship should focus on solving problems. Since more than half of Africa's population is younger than 35, there is sufficient time to include key concepts such as critical thinking and entrepreneurship in education. Finally, if someone is involved in building, selling or using AI, they should consider its impact on society (Glass, 2018).

For students to be able to observe how their studies prepare them for their careers in a workforce where they will work closely with machines, universities should collaborate with industry. University–corporate projects may provide students with the relevant experience to determine suitable careers for them. Students should further be mentored at university. If suitably matched, they could receive guidance on how to approach their careers, use technology and select suitable employers (Glass, 2018). By collaborating with educators, business leaders could ensure that the skills that students are equipped with suitably prepare them for the future workforce. Business leaders pre-empt possible changes in their organisations in preparation for suitably upskilling their workforces. CEOs will soon be expected to demonstrate the capacity for estimating this type of future scenario (Caplan, 2018)

Chatlani (2018) identifies two views about the future workforce, namely that large numbers of jobs will be lost due to automation, or that its impact will be felt gradually and that the number of affected jobs will not meet the exaggerated predictions. Some suggest that higher education may require significant changes over a short timeframe because of the impact of the information age (Pulsipher, as cited in Chatlani, 2018). Compared to previous revolutions that did not significantly affect universities' structures and organisations, the combination of technologies in AI evident in the fourth industrial revolution may impact them severely. A central concept in the progress of AI, namely deep learning, clearly encroaches on the purpose of higher education institutions because it supports new types of enhanced learning, generating new types of competition for these institutions (Gann & Dodgson, 2017).

A middle-ground approach that involves, for example, stackable degrees and partnerships also features in the automation debate. This approach suggests that students should be prepared for lifelong employability instead of predicting the obsolescence of particular jobs or the insignificance of certain majors. This steady preparation for automation appears advisable because AI may eventually mainly be responsible for routine tasks and not result in dramatic changes (Reid, as cited in Chatlani, 2018).

Aoun (2108) advises against drastic measures such as reducing the duration of qualifications because of AI's imminent impact. To adapt to advances in machine intelligence, higher education institutions should promote lifelong learning and humanics. *Humanics* prepares students for future jobs that are only suitable for human beings. It integrates technical literacies (e.g. coding and data literacy) with human literacies (e.g. creativity, ethics, cultural agility, and entrepreneurship). When combining these literacies with experiential components, students integrate their knowledge with real-life settings, resulting in deep learning (Aoun, 2018). Pulsipher (as cited in Chatlani, 2018) recommends implementing strategies such as stackable degrees and not downplaying the importance of certain degrees, for instance a bachelor's degree. All qualifications should be easily transferable and acknowledged as part of lifelong learning. People may obtain credentials and certificates over a number of years (from 10 to 20), building their scaffold of credentials. If a person obtains a qualification in a new technological field, the credential is stacked upon existing qualifications to acknowledge the value of all qualifications. Forging industry partnerships is an obvious further step that will allow higher education institutions to be responsive to industry needs.

Conclusion

The advent of AI generated considerable hopes and fears in terms of its implications for society. In terms of their fears, people appear to have some degree of choice in how they deal with the imminent changes brought about by technology. Educators, for instance, should be aware of the possible impact of AI and investigate how they could apply its possibilities to augment their teaching. And, as pointed out earlier, the experiences of various groups in terms of AI's impact will primarily depend on the decisions that various stakeholders make about implementing AI in their contexts. It has even been suggested that Africa's people and economies have a choice about whether they will take part in the technological disruption resulting from AI.

In an education context, concerns that AI tools will replace competent human educators appear to be unfounded. The focus should rather be on how AI tools could be used to reduce routine tasks, enabling educators to focus on supporting students and providing them with individual attention or focusing on their professional development. Considering the promise of AI in humanitarian areas, it appears that higher education institutions in emerging countries should focus their energy on investigating these possibilities and preparing their students in this regard. Technological disruptions such as AI often originate at universities. In considering their broader societal role, universities should investigate opportunities to prepare society for the impact of these disruptions.

Higher education institutions in an emerging-country context can never function in isolation from their environment, but they can adapt their curricula for the impact of AI and incorporate its feasible benefits in their contexts. The ultimate effect of AI is not yet clear, but some of its impacts are already evident. In the light of this, a middle-ground approach to curricular changes may be suitable, also in an emerging-country context. A further suggestion that could easily be implemented in an emerging-country context is that university–industry partnerships should be forged. Attempts are ongoing to ensure that students do not merely memorise facts and that curricula incorporate various types of assessment. It may be necessary to focus on assessing additional skills such as collaboration, creativity, data literacy, and entrepreneurship.

It appears that academic staff members will also have to be up-skilled to respond appropriately to the changes resulting from AI. If expected to encourage flexible mind-sets among students, they may also have to be exposed to this type of development. In addition, it is unlikely that academic qualifications in educators' fields of expertise will still be sufficient for guiding students in a changing world. Educators should be aware of the impact of AI on their domains of expertise, but they should also be on the lookout for general trends and prepare students for the impending changes that result from these trends. Finally, the advent of AI provides the African continent with an opportunity to serve as a breeding ground for innovation and entrepreneurship. The focus should be on establishing contextually relevant technology models and solutions that incorporate robotics and AI to the benefit of its inhabitants.

REFERENCES

Adams Becker, S., Brown, M., Dahlstrom, E., Davis, A., DePaul, K., Diaz, V. & Pomerantz, J. (2018). *NMC horizon report: 2018 higher education edition*. Louisville, CO: EDUCAUSE

Adepoju, O. (2017). Why Africa needs to prepare now for the future of work. becominghuman. ai/why-africa-needs-to-prepare-now-for-the-future-of-work-1a132e1c9a77

Albelli, H. (2018). Do classrooms hold the key to closing the skills gap? A quick guide to the role of educational institutions in creating a new workforce. edtechdigest. com/2018/10/05/do-classrooms-hold-the-key-to-closing-the-skills-gap/

Abardazzou, N. (2017). The rise of artificial intelligence in Africa. www.howwemadeitinafrica.com/rise-artificial-intelligence-africa/

Aoun, J.E. (2018). *Robot-proof: Higher education in the age of artificial intelligence*. Cambridge, MA: MIT Press.

Avedisian, A. & Matumoto, E. (2018). Three emerging technologies that will reshape education in 2019. www-edsurge-com.cdn.ampproject.org/v/s/www.edsurge.com/amp/news/2018-12-29-3-emerging-technologies-that-will-reshape-education-in-2019

Bragg, A.E. (2018). Why 'Will robots take our jobs?' is the wrong question to ask about AI. www.crainsdetroit.com/technology/why-will-robots-take-our-jobs-wrong-question-ask-about-ai

Butler-Adam J. (2018). The Fourth Industrial Revolution and education. *South African Journal of Science, 114*(5/6), Art. #a0271. doi:10.17159/sajs.2018/a0271

Business Tech. (2018). AI likely to hit South Africa harder than other countries: Expert. businesstech.co.za/news/technology/217807/ai-likely-to-hit-south-africa-harder-than-other-countries-expert/

Buthelezi, S. (2017). Imagining a decolonised 21st century education. mg.co.za/article/2017-10-06-00-imagining-a-decolonised-21st-century-education

Caplan, S. (2018). Closing the skills gap could be as simple as ABC. www.strategy-business.com/blog/Closing-the-Skills-Gap-Could-Be-as-Simple-as-ABC

Chatlani, S. (2018). Is AI disrupting higher education? www.educationdive.com/news/is-ai-disrupting-higher-education/525130/

Cheatham, B., Javanmardian,K., & Samandari, H. (2019). Confronting the risks of artificial intelligence.www.mckinsey.com/business-functions/mckinsey-analytics/our-insights/Confronting-the-risks-of-artificial-intelligence

Choudhury, K. (2018). AI in modern education. www.ami-partners.com/blog/2018/08/03/ai-in-modern-education/

Dellot, F. & Wallace-Stephens, F. (2018). A new machine age beckons and we are not remotely ready. www.thersa.org/discover/publications-and-articles/rsa-blogs/2018/11/a-new-machine-age-beckons-and-we-are-not-remotely-ready

Drabwell, C. (2018). Ethics in artificial intelligence in education: Who cares? ounews.co/education-languages-health/ethics-in-artificial-intelligence-in-education-who-cares/

EE Publishers. (2017). Artificial intelligence: Is South Africa ready? www.ee.co.za/article/artificial-intelligence-south-africa-ready.html

ESCAP. (2017). Artificial intelligence in Asia and the Pacific. www.unescap.org/resources/artificial-intelligence-asia-and-pacific

Gann, D. & Dodgson, M. (2017). How artificial intelligence will transform higher education. robohub.org/how-artificial-intelligence-will-transform-higher-education/

Gbara, L.N. (2008). *Policy analysis of Nigerian development projects, 1979–2004* (Doctoral dissertation). Retrieved from ProQuest Dissertations and Theses. (Accession Order No. 3370251).

Gillies, M. (2017). AI won't take your job, prosumers will. medium.com/human-centered-machine-learning/ai-wont-take-your-job-prosumers-will-e24151cd2d4e

Glass, S. (2018). Why universities need to prepare students for the new AI world. www.forbes.com/sites/stephanieglass/2018/07/24/why-universities-need-to-prepare-students-for-the-new-ai-world/#744b68716bc8

Gonser, S. (2018). How teens are learning crucial 'soft skills' before their internships start. www.kqed.org/mindshift/52626/how-teens-are-learning-crucial-soft-skills-before-their-internships-start

Gower, P. (2018). It's the end of the world as we know it. *Tukkie (Alumni Magazine of the University of Pretoria)*, *24* (2), 26-27.

Grover, S. (2018). The 5th 'C' of 21st Century skills? Try computational thinking (not coding). www.edsurge.com/news/2018-02-25-the-5th-c-of-21st-century-skills-try-computational-thinking-not-coding

Harper, A. (2018). Will robots replace teachers in the future? www.educationdive.com/news/will-robots-replace-teachers-in-the-future/542239/

Lachs, J. (2017). Closing the skills gap: How educators and employers can work together. www.opencolleges.edu.au/informed/features/closing-the-skills-gap-how-educators-and-employers-can-work-together/

Lambert, K. (n.d.) Could artificial intelligence replace our teachers? www.educationworld.com/could-artificial-intelligence-replace-our-teachers

Letouzé, E, & Pentland, A. (2018). Towards a human artificial intelligence for human development, *ITU Journal: ICT Discoveries*, *Special Issue*, *2*(6) Dec.

Loeffler J. (2018). Personalized learning: Artificial intelligence and education in the future. interestingengineering.com/personalized-learning-artificial-intelligence-and-education-in-the-future

Lynch, M. (2018). Will artificial intelligence disrupt higher education? www.thetechedvocate.org/will-artificial-intelligence-disrupt-higher-education/

Makhdoomi, M. (2018). Artificial Intelligence to change higher education. www.greaterkashmir.com/news/op-ed/artificial-intelligence-to-change-higher-education/285690.html

Maskey, S. (2018). AI for humanity: Using AI to make a positive impact in developing countries. www.forbes.com/sites/forbestechcouncil/2018/08/23/ai-for-humanity-using-ai-to-make-a-positive-impact-in-developing-countries-2/#627f76a91b08

Marwala, T. (2018). Opinion: Tackling bias in technology requires a new form of activism. www.uj.ac.za/newandevents/Pages/Opinion-Tackling-bias-in-technology-requires-a-new-form-of-activism.aspx

Oblinger, D.G. (2018). What will AI and robotics mean for higher education? www.ecampusnews.com/2018/08/02/what-will-ai-and-robotics-mean-for-higher-education/

Pedroncelli, P. (2018). 10 ways artificial intelligence is revolutionizing African industries. moguldom.com/166240/10-ways-artificial-intelligence-is-revolutionizing-african-industries

Popenici, S. A., & Kerr, S. (2017). Exploring the impact of artificial intelligence on teaching and learning in higher education. *Research and Practice in Technology Enhanced Learning, 12*(1), 22.

Poth, R.D. (2018). Artificial intelligence: Implications for the future of education. www.gettingsmart.com/2018/01/artificial-intelligence-implications-for-the-future-of-education/

Raymone, A.D. (2018). AI will impact 100% of jobs, professions, and industries, says IBM's Ginni Rometty. www.zdnet.com/article/ai-will-impact-100-of-jobs-professions-and-industries-says-ibms-ginni-rometty/

Seldon, A. & Abedoye, O. (2018). *The fourth education revolution: Will artificial intelligence liberate or infantilise humanity?* Buckingham: University of Buckingham Press.

Selwyn, N. (2018). Six reasons artificial intelligence technology will never take over from human teachers. www.aare.edu.au/blog/?p=2948

Tegmark, M. (2017). *Life 3.0: Being Human in the Age of Artificial Intelligence.* London: Penguin.

The Guardian. (2018). How do universities prepare graduates for jobs that don't yet exist? www.theguardian.com/education/2018/dec/20/how-do-universities-prepare-for-jobs-that-dont-yet-exist

University of Montreal. (2018). Developing AI in a responsible way. phys.org/news/2018-12-ai-responsible.html

University of Pretoria. (2018). Artificial Intelligence for Africa: An opportunity for growth, development, and democratisation. www.up.ac.za/media/shared/7/ZP_Files/ai-for-africa.zp165664.pdf

Watters, A. (2017). AI is ideological. newint.org/features/2017/11/01/audrey-watters-ai

World Economic Forum. (2016). The future of jobs: Employment, skills and workforce strategy for the fourth industrial revolution. www3.weforum.org/docs/WEF_Future_of_Jobs.pdf

Leona Ungerer is an associate professor in the Department of Industrial and Organisational Psychology at the University of South Africa (Unisa). Her areas of interest are consumer psychology and technology-mediated teaching and learning.
ungerlm@unisa.ac.za

notes

notes

Notes

Transforming higher education with a focus on integration and mastery

LISA B. BOSMAN

JULIUS C. KELLER

GARY R. BERTOLINE

What is the problem and how did we get here?

Once upon a time... college students attended class, listened to a lecture, took notes offered by the professor, went home and studied the notes, and regurgitated the memorized information in homework and exams. This cycle was completed under the pretense of 'demonstrating' enough knowledge to earn a good grade to pass the class to graduate college with a degree to get a good job to stay loyal to the same employer for their entire working career. And then, along came technology, disruptive innovations, and the global economy.

Employment was no longer bounded by loyalty to one employer, working nine-to-five jobs, or to improve the societal conditions of people within a certain state or country, so the economy changed allowing for work to take place 24/7 throughout the world. Collaboration and teamwork were no longer restricted to a physical workspace, so workers changed and became more efficient. Information was no longer limited to books and people, so a student's ability to acquire new knowledge changed instantaneously. And almost overnight, industry was demanding a new type of worker to fit the needs of the new economy, a worker who can think critically, communicate, collaborate, and solve complex open-ended problems.

No one agreed more than Holden Thorp and Buck Goldstein whose commentary in *U.S. News and World Report* (2018) stated, "Academia must recognize the importance of preparing students for the workforce." However, the authors went on to inform readers of the myriad of complexities associated with American higher education, running the gamut of limited government funding, the reality of research-focused faculty, and the public's skewed understanding associated with the ivory towers of academia. But one government funding agency, in particular, was convinced that change was needed.

The National Science Foundation (NSF), which provides approximately 27% of the total federal budget for education and research conducted in science and engineering at institutions of higher education (National Science Foundation, 2019), agreed that change was needed! In 2017, NSF worked closely with representatives from across higher education to establish strategic planning initiatives and gain reviewer recommendations for what should and shouldn't be funded, which resulted in publishing *NSF's 10 big ideas*. One of the big ideas links directly to workforce education, titled *Future of work at the human-technology frontier*, with four key research themes: building the human-technology partnership, augmenting human performance, illuminating the socio-technological landscape, and fostering lifelong learning.

Industry, government, and academia are pretty much in agreement that change is needed. But where do we go from here?

Where should we focus our efforts?

Dr. Nancy Zimpher is a senior fellow at the Rockefeller Institute of Government serving as the founding director of the nation's first Center for Education Pipeline Systems Change. She says we need to be mindful of the *new student demographic*. She suggests that the future of education starts with knowing our students and responding accordingly. Zimpher states, "The world has changed, and higher education needs to not only change with it but stay ahead of the curve, ready to receive the students who come to us. The future of education is flexibility" (Zimpher 2018).

She goes on to say, "this means expanding our operations so that we can meet students where they are, on their time. It means providing an array of avenues by which to earn a degree and support to ensure they complete."

Anant Agarwal (2018), the CEO for edX, supports this notion of providing multiple ways to complete a degree. In his recently published essay, Future-proofing higher education starts with reinventing the college degree, he tells readers we need to reinvent our education system with a focus on customizable, adaptable and flexible program offerings (2018). He suggests that our current approach to higher education is problematic, noting, "the jobs of the future will require a hybrid set of skills from a variety of subject areas. But our current education model has us spending at least three years studying the same singular discipline."

He recommends modular education as the wave of the future. In this model, modular chunks of education, obtained from a variety of educational institutions, will allow students to leverage their strengths to build the strongest foundation possible as they navigate the careers of the future. Tarandeep Singh Sekhon, a Marketing Director at KidZania and writer for BusinessWorld, follows suit with the path set forth by Zimpher and Agarwal. He provides a persuasive pitch for increased **experiential learning** as a way for educational institutions to meet future workforce needs (2018). He starts by declaring, "Skills like planning, networking, communication, adaptability, leadership, teamwork and so many more are learned through experience." He continues, "The majority of our day to day functioning is done through experience, then why do we learn from a book?"

Sekhon (2018) makes a point to recognize higher educational institutions for offering credit related to internships, co-ops, and other industry experience, but suggests there is much opportunity to incorporate a greater amount of experiential learning directly into the classroom setting. He comments about the benefits of experiential learning, noting, "This teaches them to not only be independent but when each small task is completed, they have a sense of accomplishment that can really increase their self-confidence. When they complete small tasks all by themselves, they feel empowered to do more tasks independently and efficiently."

In summary, according to workforce and education experts, some avenues related to the future of education will require adapting to the new student demographic, deploying experiential learning pedagogical approaches, and offering customizable, adaptable, and flexible learning formats. Fortunately, there is a potential solution. Many of these things can be done through competency-based education.

What is competency-based education?

"Competency-based education (CBE) is an outcome-based, student-centered form of instruction whereby students progress to more advanced work upon mastering the prerequisite content and skills (Henri, Johnson, & Nepal, 2017)." The origins of CBE date back to the early 1960s and 1970s with reforms for teacher education and the first offerings of vocational training (Nodine, 2016). Although CBE is not new, it has increasingly been receiving much attention as an inclusive pedagogical approach for meeting the needs of a more diverse student population. McDonald (2018) conducted a case study focused on adult learners, analyzing the impact of incorporating CBE self-paced mini-courses into traditional degree programs. The findings suggested an increase in student interest and motivation compared to students completing entirely self-paced CBE programs.

Bushway, Dogde, and Long (2018) provide five key hallmarks of competency-based education programs. First, time is variable, and learning is fixed. This goes against the traditional concept of the credit hour and seat time used by many academic institutions. Second, there is a required demonstration of mastery. Put simply, students cannot just show up. Instead, they need to provide evidence that a competency was obtained or mastered. Third, proficiency is determined by rigorous assessments. Assessments can be behavioral-based, knowledge-based, and portfolio-based, to name a few. But in any case, the assessment should be directly linked to the learning goals, objectives, and activities (Wiggins and McTighe, 2005). Fourth, mastery focuses on the student learning journey. In this sense, learning is not left to chance. Instead, the learning experience should be intentionally designed to focus on agency, consistency, and results. Finally, mastery is offered in a flexible and self-paced approach. Going back to the first hallmark, because time is variable and learning is fixed, academic institutions need to be aware that students learn and master subjects at different paces. Thus, the learning process needs to be flexible and allow for students to consume and master information at their own pace.

Competency-based education appears to be the perfect solution to prepare students for the future workforce. So why isn't everyone doing it?

In Amy Laitinen's (2012) report, *Cracking the credit hour*, the author provides a historical perspective on how the time-based 'Carnegie Unit' came to become the go-to protocol for establishing high school and college completion requirements. And since public funds are used to assist students in obtaining degrees, the Department of Education has also defaulted to the credit-hour system. Thus, one major issue preventing competency-based education from moving forward is the Department of Education and its current stance on regulations on Federal Student Aid programs which are authorized under the Higher Education Act, including policies and procedures related to online education and competency-based education. A big challenge to implementing competency-based education is that the Department of Education is very much reliant upon accreditation agencies to approve program offerings at higher education institutions. Unfortunately, the accreditation agencies have traditionally considered credit hours and seat time as a must for program approval. And, without accreditation, higher education institutions do not qualify for financial aid and other government assistance programs. However, it is hopeful that things will turn around soon. In April 2019, results of the Department of Education's negotiated rule-making process established language which will ultimately provide accreditors with increased flexibility to approve new and innovate types of college-level programs (Kelderman, 2019).

How can higher education get onboard with competency-based education?

Over the past decade, competency-based education has been on the rise for offering vocational education, which prepares people to work in a variety of jobs such as a craft, a trade, or as a technician. This new and innovative approach to education offers for-profit and non-profit higher education institutions, alike, an opportunity to capitalize on a business model allowing students access to self-paced, distance and online learning for completing vocational education. In these cases, competencies are commonly "obtained and demonstrated" by watching short videos, completing assignments, and passing an online assessment demonstrating the students' ability to accomplish a series of learning objectives.

However, little progress has taken place, and few resources exist that show how to incorporate competency-based education into traditional bachelor's degree programs. Purdue University is one exception. Dean Gary Bertoline recently received approval for a new strategic approach to education called the Ten Elements of Transformation affirming, "We needed to prepare graduates who not only have deep technical skills but who also are innovators and 'makers,' with an attitude of curiosity to learn and connect with others, and the courage to initiate and collaborate for the benefit of society. Further, we need to recognize the importance of humanities and social science studies and integrate those with technology studies (https://polytechnic.purdue.edu/transformation)." The *Ten elements of transformation* include: theory-based applied learning, team project-based learning, modernized teaching methods, integrated learning-in-context curriculum, integrated humanities studies, senior capstone projects, internships, global and cultural immersions, faculty-to-student mentorship, and competency credentialing.

Purdue University's new strategic focus on the *Ten elements of transformation* has resulted in the design and implementation of a new B.S. in Transdisciplinary Studies in Technology, offered through the Purdue Polytechnic Institute (formerly, the College of Engineering Technology). This degree is innovative, experimental, and meets all goals set forward by the Transformation. However, three things are noteworthy as they are innovative for Purdue and higher education in general.

First, it is competency-based in that students are required to show mastery of meeting 20 core competencies. This is done qualitatively through one-on-one feedback with faculty mentors. The B.S. in Transdisciplinary Studies in Technology program has 20 competencies belonging to the five major competency clusters of Create and Innovate, Interact with Others, Inquire and Analyze, Communicate, and Engage in Culture, Values and the Arts. It requires students to demonstrate mastery of meeting core competencies through submission of an artifact to show the 'doing' and submission of a reflection to demonstrate the 'thinking.' Mastery is obtained through demonstrating the 'doing' and thinking a minimum of three times throughout the first three years of the program where each time students are required to compare and contrast the new experience from the previous experience. Then, during the two-semester senior capstone, students independently drive and incorporate the competencies into the final capstone project. This integrated approach to competency-based education will culminate with a competency defense, similar to that completed during the thesis or dissertation process.

Second, it is transdisciplinary in that learning experiences integrate the humanities into engineering, design, and technology skill sets through design and portfolio courses. Each semester students engage in a substantial reading list of short books and narratives, applying the concepts to a human-centered design project, and showcase the learning experience through reflections and an ePortfolio. Each semester follows a theme; past themes have included Play, Transportation, Renewable Energy, and Food. The B.S. in Transdisciplinary

Studies in Technology program is transdisciplinary, and although it is housed within the Polytechnic, it offers learning experiences which integrate the humanities into engineering, design, and technology skill sets. This is done for students through a requirement to enroll and complete six credits of design studio labs ('doing') and three credits of portfolio ('reflective thinking') each academic school year. Transdisciplinary education offers a holistic perspective for considering approaches to problem-solving typical of those in the workforce existing at the intersection of domains and disciplines, where commonality identification is required to produce something new and unique.

Finally, about one-third of the required credits are 'free credits.' The B.S. in Transdisciplinary Studies in Technology degree requires a minimum of 120 credits. About 1/3 of the credits are general education courses, about 1/3 of the credits are core courses including the design studio labs and portfolio courses, and the remaining approximate 1/3 of the required credits are "free credits" in that students are given agency to customize their own educational journey. The 'free credits' go beyond the traditional notion of electives to allow students to select a series of pathways in coursework offered throughout the entire university. The benefit of customized education pathways is that it allows students the freedom and flexibility to design and define their own path, focusing on their individual strengths to empower them towards optimization of their future workforce potential.

Now What?

According to Rachel Gorton, instructional technology coordinator, critical conversations are the necessary starting point (Bengfort, 2018). She states, "One piece of advice for others is not to shy away from those conversations; they're integral to making a successful plan and ensuring that all students can be successful." Gorton continues, "Be willing to examine everything. We looked at the classes we were offering to students; we looked at the time and space and how students are moving through their day and their year and their education as a whole; we looked at where they're going next and how we are preparing them. It's a big shift, but it's always very, very rewarding."

In conclusion, we leave with several areas for reevaluation. Higher education should reconsider...

- their value proposition in what they have to offer incoming students.
- the promotion and tenure process and the relative weights placed on research, teaching, and service.
- education from an ecosystem perspective, taking into consideration industry, government, accreditation agencies, alumni, the local community, and global society as a whole.
- their target stakeholders and approach to meeting stakeholder needs.
- the role of competency-based education in its efforts to broaden participation, increase enrollment and completion rates, provide a more inclusive teaching and learning environment, and develop educational programs meeting the workforce needs of the future.

REFERENCES

Agarwal, A. (2018, November). Future-proofing higher education starts with reinventing the college degree. *The future of college.* qz.com/1469291/future-proofing-higher-education-starts-with-reinventing-the-college-degree/

Bengfort, J. (2018, November). Q&A: Rachel Gorton on how K-12 schools envision the future of education. *EdTech focus on K-12.* edtechmagazine.com/k12/article/2018/11/qa-rachel-gorton-how-k-12-schools-envision-future-education

Dodge, L., Bushway, D. J., & Long, C. S. (2018). *A leader's guide to competency-based education: From inception to implementation.* Sterling, VA: Stylus Publishing, LLC.

Henri, M., Johnson, M. D., & Nepal, B. (2017). A review of competency-based learning: Tools, assessments, and recommendations. *Journal of Engineering Education, 106,* 607-638.

Kelderman, E. (2019, April). Consensus or chaos? Education Dept.'s rule-making session reaches agreement. *The Chronicle of Higher Education*. www. chronicle.com/article/Consensus-or-Chaos-Education/246064

Laitinen, A. (2012, September). Cracking the credit hour. *New America Foundation*. www. newamerica.org/education-policy/policy-papers/cracking-the-credit-hour/

McDonald, N.A. (2018). A private, nonprofit university's experiences designing a competency-based degree for adult learners. *Journal of Continuing Higher Education*, 66(1), 34-45. doi:10.1080/0737736 3.2018.1415632

National Science Foundation. (2019, February). Fact Sheet. www.nsf. gov/news/news_summ.jsp?cntn_ id=100595

Nodine, T.R. (2016). How did we get here? A brief history of competency-based higher education in the United States. *The Journal of Competency-Based Education*, 1(1), 5-11. doi:10.1002/ cbe2.1004

Sekhon, T.S. (2018, December). Experiential learning as the future of education. *Business World*. www. businessworld.in/article/Experiential-Learning-As-The-Future-Of-Education/15-12-2018-165152/

Thorp, H., & Goldstein, B. (2018, November). Time for a truce between higher ed and the public. *U.S. News and World Report*. www.usnews. com/news/education-news/ articles/2018-11-30/its-time-for-a-truce-between-higher-education-and-the-public

Wiggins, G.P., & McTighe, J. (2005). *Understanding by design*. Alexandria, VA: ASCD Publications.

Zimpher, N. (Producer). (2018, November 28). The future of higher education is flexibility. *The New York Academy of Sciences*. www.nyas. org/magazines/imagining-the-next-100-years/the-future-of-higher-education-is-flexibility/

Lisa B. Bosman is an assistant professor in the Department of Technology Leadership and Innovation at Purdue University. She has a Ph.D. in Industrial Engineering and an extensive background in education research methods. Her STEM education research interests include the entrepreneurial mindset, competency-based learning, self-regulated learning, transdisciplinary education, civic engagement, and faculty professional development. lbosman@purdue.edu

Julius C. Keller is an assistant professor in the School of Aviation and Transportation Technology at Purdue University. He is an active Certified Flight Instructor with airplane single- and multi-engine, and instrument-airplane ratings. He leads the proficiency efforts related aviation curriculum. Keller64@purdue.edu

Gary R. Bertoline is the dean of the Purdue Polytechnic Institute at Purdue University. His research interests are in scientific visualization, interactive immersive environments, distributed and grid computing, workforce education and STEM education, where he has particular interests in educational transformation. bertolig@purdue.edu

notes

notes

....

....

....

....

....

....

....

....

....

....

....

....

....

....

....

notes

notes

Institutionalizing community engagement in higher education: The community engagement institute

AUDREY FALK

RUSSELL OLWELL

Introduction and overview of community engagement in higher education

Across the United States and internationally, institutions of higher education are deepening their commitment to community engagement through a broad range of practices and approaches. The Carnegie Elective Classification in Community Engagement, initiated in 2006, recognizes colleges and universities for their institutionalization of community engagement, and this process serves as a motivation for many campus-wide community engagement efforts (Saltmarsh & Johnson, 2018). The Talloires Network, initiated in 2005, is an international organization comprised of member institutions which are committed to the civic purposes of higher education (Tufts University, 2018), and has grown to include 379 institutional members which represent 77 countries and a total student enrollment of over six million. The Coalition of Urban and Metropolitan Universities, an institutional membership organization dedicated to urban engagement, reports a current membership of over 90 member institutions (n.d.). The publication of A crucible moment in 2012 represented a national call to action regarding higher education community engagement. The movement toward recognizing, valuing, and validating community engagement in higher education is continuing to gain momentum.

Growth in community engagement is not limited to higher education. Community engagement is increasingly practiced in PreK-12 school settings and nonprofit organizations, and they also practice many of its central concepts and techniques in fields such as public health and philanthropy. However, there is no one common, shared, agreed-upon definition of community engagement. One frequently cited definition of community engagement is that put forth by the Centers for Disease Control and Prevention (CDC, 1997). In this definition, community engagement is, "...the process of working collaboratively with and through groups of people affiliated by geographic proximity, special interest, or similar situations to address issues affecting the well-being of those people" (p. 9; as cited in Clinical and Translational Science Awards Consortium,, 2011, p. 3). This definition is consistent with our view of community engagement. We view community engagement as interaction and purposeful activity which aims to facilitate positive changes in individuals and communities and may or may not include institutions of higher education.

In higher education, community engagement is typically defined narrowly as community outreach and partnership wherein institutions of higher education are central and necessary players and actors. For example, the elective Carnegie Classification uses the following definition: "community engagement describes the collaboration between institutions of higher education and their larger communities (local, regional/state, national, global) for the mutually beneficial exchange of knowledge and resources in a context of partnership and reciprocity" (Brown University Swearer Center, n.d.).

Comparing the Carnegie Classification definition and the CDC definition, we see startling contrasts. The CDC definition describes a process of working with and through groups of people who represent different types of communities, such as communities of place and communities of interest, toward the betterment of those people and communities. The Carnegie definition focuses, alternatively, on higher education's engagement with communities, and the emphasis shifts from community betterment to mutuality and reciprocity.

On one hand, it is natural that the institution of higher education will consider community engagement from the vantage point of campus-community engagement. On the other hand, the academy could better serve communities by thinking about how they can support community engagement, broadly defined. Decentralizing the role of higher education is important for many reasons. It helps to minimize power imbalances between higher education institutions and community partners. It helps to maintain the focus on community improvement. It legitimizes the involvement of institutional partners other than higher education institutions.

Regarding the reciprocity and mutuality component of the Carnegie Classification definition, which is entirely absent from the CDC's definition of community engagement, again, we offer competing perspectives. In one way, we acknowledge that true engagement must have some component of mutual benefit. People and institutions immerse themselves in activities that are, on some level, self-serving. There are a whole range of benefits we may derive from community engagement as individuals, from a personal sense of satisfaction to resume-building and networking, from learning skills to making friends. Institutions benefit from community engagement through public relations, marketing, and branding. In many cases, community engagement is intricately tied with an organization's mission, thereby making communication engagement work central to their cause.

In another way, the primary aim of community engagement is not a self-serving one. It is community improvement. That is the reason for community engagement. Other benefits and outcomes are secondary.

Where do we land then on this question of whether reciprocity and mutuality belong in a definition of community engagement? We land on the side of inclusion of mutuality, if not in the definition, certainly in the principles of community engagement. We do so not from a strategic gain perspective, whereby each participant engages for what he or she will get out of the experience. Rather, we do so because of our belief in the transformative power of community engagement. From an educational and human development perspective, we believe that community engagement is a mutually beneficial process which supports the individual growth and transformation of all involved. Community engagement is not about charity, but partnership and alliance. The process of community engagement consists of creating and nurturing partnerships through which there are learning and growth opportunities for all participants, whether they are students, researchers, public health professionals, nonprofit leaders, or community members.

The Carnegie Classification definition of community engagement may be viewed as an attempt to operationalize, for higher education's purposes, the broader definition of community engagement, such as that offered by the CDC. However, most practitioners in higher education only see the Carnegie-type definitions and are unaware of the broader definition of community engagement. This is deeply problematic. Higher education community engagement is simply community engagement which involves colleges or universities as partners.

Having a special definition of higher education community engagement has the potential to be unhelpful. Institutions of higher education are one partner among many, working alongside community members and community groups and organizations to forward expressed community goals. Having a special definition can take the pressure off of higher education to actualize community engagement. Institutions of higher education risk diverting attention from community needs and goals to an unbalanced prioritization of students' learning and institutional agendas. As a case in point, Ross and Stoecker

(2016) highlight academia's focus on evaluation of the learning objectives of college students' service-learning experiences rather than the assessment of community outcomes. They observe, "The lack of focus on community outcomes also appears in our definitions" (p. 9).

There are many ways that institutions of higher education participate in community engagement, such as service-learning, community-university partnerships, and community-engaged research. However, college and university faculty, staff, and administrators need to analyze whether their practices of community engagement align with a broader focus on collaboration and partnership with communities that neither centralizes nor prioritizes the contributions or needs of higher education institutions. With the onus on community processes and community well-being rather than on student learning or campus interests, some of our community engagement practices may not be meeting their full potential.

Higher education's roots in community engagement are deep. These include philosophical orientations toward community engagement work and practical applications. For example, we can trace back community engagement from an intellectual perspective to the philosophical work of John Dewey (1944; 1997) who viewed experience as critical to education, and education as foundational to democracy. Giles and Eyler (1994) articulated the connections between Dewey's principles, such as continuity and interaction in experience and learning, and academic service-learning. Settlement houses provided early opportunities for college students and faculty to engage with immigrants and communities and Jane Addams, founder of Hull House, is also recognized as a pioneer of service-learning in practice (Daynes & Longo, 2004). Settlement houses afforded students the opportunity to engage in organizing and research activities while deepening their understanding of complex social and political issues. The roots of community engagement are also in the intellectual and activist work of Paulo Freire (2006), who sought to engage the disenfranchised in their liberation through a process of reflection, meaning-making, and action. The academy has long been a space for student organizing for civil rights.

Benefits of community engagement

Community engagement intends to address community issues. The actual issues addressed are too far-reaching and numerous to mention, but include issues such as poverty, homelessness, health and wellness, mental health, and education. Without ignoring the reality of genuine need in a community, community engagement efforts draw on asset-based perspectives, seeing the potential for leadership and change coming from within the community. Community engagement has a social justice lens, and human well-being and community wellness are connected with issues of equity, access, power, and privilege. Community engagement is intended to build upon and further develop community resources, which includes addressing challenges such as access, equity, capacity, and infrastructure.

In public health, we see significant attention in the literature to the community outcomes of engagement. For example, of 24 studies that met criteria for inclusion in Cyril, Smith, Possamai-Inesedy, and Renzaho's (2015) meta-analysis of community engagement as a health intervention for disadvantaged populations, 87.5% of the studies resulted in health benefits for participants, such as access, information, and positive behavior change. Lam et al.'s (2016) study of community engagement benefits for depressed low-income individuals showed a positive impact in mental health but not in other areas. As noted earlier, in the arena of higher education, the scholarship reporting benefits to the community is limited.

Community engagement is believed to support student development in a wide range of dimensions. Eyler and Giles' (1999) seminal text, Where's the learning in service-learning?, suggested that service-learning impacts college students' personal and interpersonal growth, application of course content, interest in and reflection on complex social issues, critical thinking skills, perspective-taking, and civic identity. Furthermore, community engagement is believed to enhance student engagement and retention. Since the research on community engagement suggests that with the right methodology, the impact can be positive, how do we align campus programs to have the maximum impact both on and off-campus? How do we educate faculty, staff, and students to conceive community engagement more broadly and to think about their community engagement practices differently? How can higher education support community engagement rather than attempt to co-opt or drive community engagement?

The Community Engagement Institute

I, Audrey Falk, the lead author of this chapter, attended a faculty institute on community engagement at the University of Notre Dame (UND) in summer 2017. I am the Director of the Community Engagement Master's Program at Merrimack College. I had found and applied to the UND institute online as it was well-aligned with my program and professional and scholarly interests. The institute is an annual program offered by the Center for Social Concerns at UND. The program was three days in length and included information, networking, site visits, and reflection. Attendees were primarily faculty and staff from UND and other local institutions. The program impressed me and I felt that it could be replicated, or modelled, after, at our institution, Merrimack College.

Rationale and Goals

Despite the numerous potential benefits of campus community engagement, there are many challenges to the institutionalization of community engagement and effective practice within higher education. In particular, there are concerns that community engagement is embraced by segments or pockets of an institution's faculty and students but not holistically embraced by the entire institution. Even institutions that are viewed as models of community engagement can be found, when studied in more depth, to have multiple definitions and ideas about community engagement co-existing on campus (Starke, et al., 2017).

Integrating community engagement efforts across a campus is an example of a challenging campus change. Kezar (2009) describes campuses as brimming with change initiatives, often unconnected, and more likely missing opportunities for synergy on campus. Kezar writes, "Campus leaders need to create mechanisms to connect faculty or staff with similar ideas. Networks, informed groups, and collaboratives can secure more buy-in for ideas and make similar projects more viable by creating more allies across campus to support them, synergies among them, and broader leadership for them" (p. 20).

While Merrimack College has an extensive array of community engagement projects, they are led by different divisions and offices, which can have very distinct and diverging visions of the goals and outcomes of community engagement. As a Catholic institution, many of our community engagement efforts are executed from a mission and ministry perspective, which may have substantial differences from programs run with a community engagement philosophy. We hoped that by hosting the Community Engagement Institute, we could raise awareness of community engagement initiatives occurring across the college, in different schools, departments, and disciplines. We hoped that our program would be motivating, inspirational, and informative for those already doing community engagement work and for those who might be open to experimenting with the practice. We viewed the Community Engagement Institute as a vehicle to break down departmental and discipline silos and move toward interdisciplinary approaches.

Within the college context, the institute sought to bring together both grassroots faculty and students involved in programs, as well as administrators (such as the Provost, Vice-Provosts and Deans) who can support and fund these initiatives. Thus, this effort sought to bring together participants to develop the synergies that Kezar describes as lost opportunities, both between different levels of the college and between the college and the community.

Aware of the inherent power structures inherent in community engagement work, we sought to have an institute that was inclusive and welcoming and valued the participation of people with different knowledge and expertise pertinent to community engagement. We wanted the institute to being attended by and directly valuable for community members and representatives of community organizations. We wanted community input regarding the focus, content, and structure of the institute.

We sought to break down walls between campus and community and to move toward reciprocity and mutual benefit in partnership relationships. Thus, the Community Engagement Institute sought to bring together individuals both from within and outside the college. We sought to create an environment that valued all participants, through having panels that highlighted the experiences and recommendations of community organizations.

We saw the Community Engagement Institute as a training and professional development opportunity for all participants. We felt it was important to involve our community engagement graduate students as they are the future leaders of the community engagement field in higher education, nonprofit, school, and community contexts. We wished to build up students, particularly graduate students in community engagement, by engaging them in dialogue about best practices and fostering a culture of inclusivity and transparency. We also believed that our community engagement students could provide valuable information, resources, and perspectives to other attendees. Hopefully, students would see the initiative as valuable, and bring this activity to their future community or campus careers.

In sum, the Community Engagement Institute sought to bring together a diverse group of individuals within the college and in the community to network, share ideas, reflect on best practices, and strategize about how we can best institutionalize, operationalize, and implement community engagement work.

Planning Process

Merrimack College is a private, Catholic and Augustinian college in Massachusetts, with a long tradition of serving community needs. I, Audrey Falk, talked with colleagues about the possibility of having a Community Engagement Institute at Merrimack College with colleagues shortly after returning from the institute at UND. First, I reached out to a few colleagues, including Russ Olwell, Associate Dean of the School of Education and Social Policy and second author of this chapter; Patricia Sendall, who was at the time the Dean of Experiential Education; Mary McHugh, Executive Director of Civic and Community Engagement; and Laura Hillier, Director of Community Partnerships for the School of Education and Social Policy.

Based upon this outreach, we held a meeting early in September 2017 which included the same group identified above and Kathryn Nielsen, Associate Provost and Director of Strategic Initiatives. At this meeting, I talked about my experiences at the UND institute and shared ideas regarding developing a similar program for Merrimack College. I received positive feedback and was encouraged to follow up with the Dean of the School of Education and Social Policy, who was also supportive.

Soon thereafter, I established a team drive for these and a few additional individuals to have access to drafts of a program for Merrimack College. Around the same time, in late October 2017, Merrimack College hosted a Planning Institute of the World Association for Cooperative Education (WACE) which was attended by many faculty and staff members from different schools in the college who shared interests pertinent to experiential education and service-learning. At this meeting, Sendall and I discussed the potential value of having the Merrimack College Center for Excellence in Teaching and Learning (CETL) take a lead role in the planning and implementation of the institute.

Nielsen, who serves as Associate Provost, also oversees CETL and was already involved in these discussions. Nielsen continue to express support. Through discussions between Nielsen, the Dean of the School of Education and Social Policy, and the Provost, by early January, we had received confirmation that there was a high level of support for a program that would be a dinner event plus a full day.

Nielsen suggested that the next step was to engage a larger group of individuals from across the college in a discussion about the institute to ensure that there was enough buy-in across disciplines and colleges. Thus, we created a list of about individuals, primarily faculty, from across the college who had projects and initiatives in the community. We were also intentional about including community members at this meeting. We invited several individuals from the community, including community partners and alumni of the Master's Program in Community Engagement. The meeting was held on Valentine's Day and was thus promoted as a planning event "for the love of community." We extended about 25 invitations, and about half of those invited attended, including the directors of two local nonprofit organizations that are close collaborators with the college. A draft agenda was distributed to attendees, and they provided support for the initiative as well as feedback regarding the content and structure of the event. There was a lot of discussion about the best timeframe for the event and how to incentivize diverse and broad participation.

Building support across the schools and offices at the college was a critical task. Newer faculty across campus, but particularly in the health sciences, might be involved in research or service activities in the community, but might not be connected to existing service initiatives. Thus, reaching out to newer colleagues could help both bolster the work of those faculty members and create connections to foster interdisciplinary collaboration on key projects. We recruited faculty and administrators across all five of our schools, and across areas such as Student Affairs, Mission and Ministry, and Service Learning.

Once we had the buy-in from the larger group and financial commitment from the institution, we, the two authors of this chapter, orchestrated the planning and implementation of the event with support from Nielsen. He took the lead on logistical matters and we reached out to the potential speakers and to communicate a vision for the program. We also reached out to Campus Compact of Southern New England, which served as a co-sponsor of the institute and assisted with external promotion and outreach.

Timing

While this was a pilot, we were intentional about our purposes and our vision for the program. We knew we had the budget and commitment for a dinner event and a full day. We decided that we wanted the dinner event to serve as a kick-off to the program and we wanted it to be festive and celebratory. We saw this event as an opportunity to celebrate our collective success and effort in regard to community engagement work. We decided to hold this event at the end os f a day on which the college hosted an experiential education workshop as a way of tying the two programs together. The full-day institute took place the next day.

The scheduling of the program for the end of May had other benefits for us. Our hope was to include as many of the Community Engagement graduate students as possible. Most students in the Community Engagement Program complete the program in twelve months, beginning and ending in May. Thus, by holding the program in late May, we could include both incoming and graduating or just-graduated students.

Additionally, faculty had completed their spring courses, but they were still on contract. We hoped that the scheduling would make the institute accessible for those interested in attending. One factor that encouraged us to move forward on the workshop was the arrival on campus of many new faculty over the past three years, who might have an interest, but little formal training, in community engagement. The newly created School of Health Sciences had hired many new faculty members with interest in public and community health programs, and the School of Education and Social Policy had hired new faculty eager to connect to schools in the community.

Program

We held the evening event in the atrium of the college's theatre. The program began with an address by the provost who also gave a brief address at the beginning of the daylong program. We had decided that the provost's contribution was important to demonstrate the deep commitment of the institution to community engagement. To maintain our focus on students and their role in community engagement, the dinner program featured recognition of the college's 2018 Newman Civic Fellow. The Newman Civic Fellowship is a program of Campus Compact that provides training, networking, and mentoring opportunities for undergraduate and graduate students who are committed to community engagement.

We also used the evening as a chance to highlight the emerging Early College program at Merrimack College, created in partnership with Lawrence Public Schools. This program brings over 150 juniors and seniors in a local, high-needs urban high school to campus every day to take college classes. In partnership with the district, students earn up to 16 college credits, free to the students and families, with the aim of helping these students view college as a part of their future.

Early college panelists, including faculty, administrators, and students involved in dual enrollment initiatives at Merrimack College or other local institutions, spoke about their experiences in dual enrollment and the value of this campus-community partnership. A student enrolled in the program spoke about her experience in the program, and how it gave her confidence in herself, and pride in her community. The president of a local community college spoke about his institution's role in the early college initiative in Lawrence. His presence and involvement demonstrated and highlighted the importance of cross-institution cooperation in community engagement.

The day-long program included a morning panel of community partners. We planned to get community partners up to the front of the room as often as possible during the day, as they often lose their voices in the din of academic debate and discussion. Two community organizations were represented on the morning panel, including an organization that offers food pantries and the provision of other basic needs to low-income individuals and families and a local independent living community for senior citizens. These organizational representatives spoke directly to the needs of the community, and the needs of their organizations. The speakers discussed their organizations, partnerships with Merrimack College and other institutions, and continuing needs, desired partnerships, or other ideas for future collaboration.

Andrew Seligsohn, the President of Campus Compact, gave an inspiring talk focused on the importance of community engagement. He framed the field by talking about the relationship between higher education institutions serving as a strong and just anchor in their community and building community and civic engagement among an institution's own students. Seligsohn forcefully made the case that having one aspect— student engagement or being a good anchor in the community—was less powerful without the other. This message helped participants see that their own work, with students or institutionally, is part of a larger campus-wide/community agenda, and that unconnected efforts miss the possibility of having a broader impact.

A panel composed of faculty and their partners focused on key faculty-led initiatives at the college. The Financial Capability Center, which is a program that engages college business students as financial coaches for local low-income families, included representation on the panel by the program director, a nonprofit partner, and a graduate student fellow. Also represented on the panel were faculty members from the School of Education and Social Policy and the School of Science and Engineering engaged in science-based initiatives with local youth. The panelists described the development and evolution of these programs and critical challenges and strategies for success. They spoke of the difficulties of this work, and how the work needed to pivot to meet changing local needs.

Lunch included an engaging discussion led by one of the Augustinian priests of Merrimack College, focusing on both where community engagement can uplift a community, and where it might serve to maintain oppression. This discussion provided an opportunity for reflection on the connections between our community engagement work and our values and personal missions.

Breakout sessions provided a chance for participants to dive deeper into an area that interested them. The breakout choices were on doing reflection well; diversity and cultural competence in community engagement; and partnering with your campus serving learning or civic engagement center. A mix of individuals including a faculty member, a staff member, an adjunct instructor who is also a community agency leader, and a staff member of a local community college led the breakout sessions.

Next, participants came back together for a discussion of the Carnegie Classification process. This was a timely discussion as the college is applying for the Carnegie Classification. Elaine Ward, a faculty member in the School of Education and Social Policy and an expert in community engagement, provided an overview of the classification process, and how campuses can use the process to develop stronger community engagement programs. This included a discussion of the purposes of the classification and its value and importance for the institutionalization of community engagement on college campuses.

In keeping with the UND program, it was important to us that the institute include opportunities for being physically present in the community. We planned three site visits to local organizations. One of these was Hands to Help which is an outreach arm of Merrimack College. It is housed in a former school building in Lawrence and its primary initiative is an after school tutoring and homework help program staffed by Merrimack College students. SquashBusters was another site visit option. SquashBusters operates in Boston, Providence, and Lawrence. The program engages youth in the sport of squash while also promoting high school graduation and college access. It is connected with similar programs throughout the country under the umbrella of the national organization, Squash and Education Alliance. SquashBusters has a strong partnership with the Master's Program in Community Engagement through an initiative we call Lawrence2College. Through this program, they involve community engagement students in supporting SquashBusters youth in Lawrence as they apply for college. The third site visit that was planned was to the Lawrence YMCA, where the college has an Active Science partnership through which youth engage in physical activity and learn about exercise science. The program itinerary culminated with dinner at a local cafe in Lawrence.

Lessons Learned and Recommendations

Attendance at the Community Engagement Institute was strong. Between the two days, roughly one hundred people were in attendance, including Merrimack College faculty, staff, and graduate students, and community members and representatives of local community organizations and other institutions of higher education. We advertised the institute through Campus Compact and through our networks and there were also several alumni and representatives of other local institutions of higher education in attendance. The mix of people at the institution was diverse, and the presenters were very informative and interesting. Participants were highly engaged and seemed to appreciate the information they received, the networking opportunities, and the positive attention to community engagement.

At the most basic level, the Community Engagement Institute brought attention to community engagement from individuals across the campus. It was a demonstration of the college's commitment to community engagement work. The institution provided a vehicle for bringing together members of the campus community and the local community who are committed to partnership and engagement work. The institute generated useful discussions about how we ought to continue and deepen this work.

Evaluation of the institute showed that participants found the topics valuable for their own work. Of the twenty participants who completed the six-item evaluation questionnaire, the vast majority found that the institute provided useful information and strategies; provided a valuable opportunity to meet others at the college, from other institutions, and in the community; and gave participants ideas for their own work (all these items scored over ninety percent strongly agree or agree). More participants found talks by lead speakers, the faculty panel, and the community partner panels productive (over eighty percent strongly agree or agree). Breakout sessions, tours, and meals were all rated well, with over fifty percent finding each valuable, but less satisfying to participants. Ironically, all the more didactic on-campus workshops were evaluated more favorably than any of the activities that got participants off campus and into the community.

Attendance at sessions told a similar story. While the institute was generally well-attended, the site visits and the community dinner were less well attended than the workshop sessions. While the planners limited the number of sites visited to three, each site received fewer visitors than expected, and one site had only one visitor. As the planners of the institute, we felt that the time in the community was perhaps the most important part of the program. We would like to continue to offer the site visits while considering what we can do to ensure more participation in them. Perhaps reversing the order of the day, beginning with community tours might help bring a more participant focus on community as the initial starting point for this work.

An institute such as this is a conversation starter. We hope that the institute can become an annual event that will help to keep the conversation about community engagement alive on our campus and in our community throughout the year.

Community engagement as connector

Too often, higher education community engagement efforts replicate the problems seen in the rest of the university - divided and disconnected efforts of a multitude of offices and programs, sometimes purporting to serve the same participants at the same time. Recent attempts to align community engagement efforts, through the Carnegie Community Engagement process, or through Campus Compact programming, have gone a long way on many campuses to convening key stakeholders, and setting common goals. However, almost any campus will benefit from holding cross-campus activities such as a Community Engagement Institute to better define community engagement, and the campus will strengthen its bond with invited community partners.

Community engagement is inherently interdisciplinary and has the potential to involve faculty and students from all disciplines. Thus, it has great potential to be a unifying force within a college or university, connecting individuals and departments with one another in ways they may not have previously connected. Thus, the practice of working with communities outside the campus can have the benefit of also building community within the campus. Through the institute we held at Merrimack College, we met faculty and staff doing community engagement work, some of whom we had not previously had contact with.

Community engagement is intended to foster social change. By convening community members, graduate students, staff, and faculty together for shared dialogue and exchange regarding best practices, challenges, and opportunities in community engagement, relationships develop, and power dynamics are interrogated. Community members and graduate students can share their expertise which is valued and appreciated.

Potential benefits of a Community Engagement Institute include inspiring creativity and innovation through new service learning and experiential education courses, partnerships, and initiatives. Community engagement supports a wide range of important higher education issues such as higher education access, student engagement and retention, and relevance. It is foundational to transformational learning and social justice on college campuses and in communities.

This chapter was completed during Audrey Falk's sabbatical from Merrimack College. Audrey would like to acknowledge Merrimack College's support of her sabbatical. Additionally, Northern Essex Community College provided an office space to Audrey for the duration of her sabbatical. The support of Northern Essex Community College is greatly appreciated.

REFERENCES

Brown University Swearer Center. (n.d.) Defining community engagement. www.brown.edu/swearer/carnegie/about

Clinical and Translational Science Awards Consortium, Community Engagement Key Function Committee Task Force on the Principles of Community Engagement. (2011). *Principles of community engagement* (2nd ed.). Bethesda, MD: National Institutes of Health. www.atsdr.cdc.gov/communityengagement/pdf/PCE_Report_508_FINAL.pdf

Coalition of Urban and Metropolitan Universities. (n.d.) CUMU members. www.cumuonline.org/cumu-members/

Cyril, S., Smith, B.J., Possamai-Inesedy, A., & Renzaho, A.M.N. (2015). *Exploring the role of community engagement in improving the health of disadvantaged populations: A systematic review.* Global Health Action. doi:10.3402/gha.v8.29842

Daynes, G., & Longo, N.V. (2004). Jane Addams and the origins of service-learning practice in the United States. *Michigan Journal of Community Service Learning, 11*(1), 5-13.

Dewey, J. (1944). *Democracy and education.* New York: The Free Press.

Dewey, J. (1997). *Experience and education.* New York: Touchstone.

Eyler, J., & Giles, D.G. (1999). *Where's the learning in service-learning?* San Francisco, CA: Jossey-Bass.

Friere, P. (2006). *Pedagogy of the oppressed: 30th anniversary edition.* New York: Continuum.

Giles, D., & Eyler, J. (1994). The theoretical roots of service-learning in John Dewey: Toward a theory of service-learning. *Michigan Journal of Community Service Learning, 1*(1), 77-85.

Kezar, A. (2009). Change in higher education: Not enough, or too much? *Change,* (6), 18-23. doi:10.1080/00091380903270110

Lam, C.A., Sherbourne, C., Tang, L., Belin, T.R., Williams, P., Young-Brinn, A., & Wells, K.B. (2016). The impact of community engagement on health, social, and utilization outcomes in depressed, impoverished populations: Secondary findings from a randomized trial. *Journal of the American Board of Family Medicine, 29*(3), 325-338.

The National Task Force on Civic Learning and Democratic Engagement. (2012). A *crucible moment: College learning and democracy's future.* Washington, DC: Association of American Colleges and Universities.

Ross, J.A., & Stoecker, R. (2016). The emotional context of higher education community engagement. *Journal of Community Engagement and Scholarship, 9*(2), 7-18.

Saltmarsh, J., & Johnson, M.B. (Eds). (2018). *The Elective Carnegie Community Engagement Classification: Constructing a successful application for first-time and re-classification applicants.* Boston, MA: Campus Compact.

Starke, A. Shenouda, K., Smith-Howell, D. (2017) Conceptualizing community engagement: Starting a campus wide dialogue *Metropolitan Universities, 28*(2) (Spring), DOI: 10.18060/21515

Stoecker, R. (2016). *Liberating service learning and the rest of higher education civic engagement.* Philadelphia: Temple University Press.

Tufts University. (2018). Who we are. talloiresnetwork.tufts.edu/who-we-are

Audrey Falk is an associate professor and director of the Master's Program in Community Engagement at Merrimack College.
falka@merrimack.edu

Russell Olwell is associate dean of the School of Education and Social Policy at Merrimack College.
olwellr@merrimack.edu

Notes

Notes

....

....

....

....

....

....

....

....

....

....

....

....

....

....

....

NOTES

notes

Virtual communities of practice in the future of education

SILVIA CECILIA ENRÍQUEZ

SANDRA BEATRIZ GARGIULO

MARÍA JIMENA PONZ

ERICA ELENA SCORIANS

Introduction: *Docentes en línea,* a Virtual Community of Practice

The authors of this chapter are founding members and part of the directing staff of *Docentes en línea* (Online teachers, *Del*), a virtual community of practice (VCoP) belonging to the Universidad Nacional de La Plata, Argentina (National University of La Plata, UNLP), which was created in 2012 and began its public activity in 2013. The term *community of practice* (CoP), coined by Lave and Wenger in 1991, has more recently been defined as "...groups of people who share a concern or a passion for something they do and learn how to do it better as they interact regularly" (Wenger-Trayner, 2015). They aim at making tacit knowledge explicit and can, like in our case, be a knowledge stewarding community (Dale, 2009).

Leaving aside the discussion of finer points as to their characteristics, VCoPs (also called Online CoPs) are CoPs that make use of technology, and are therefore in need of technology stewarding, which Wenger, White, and Smith (2009) define: "As more communities choose technologies to help them be together, a distinct function emerges to attend to this interplay between technology and the community: we call it *technology stewarding* to suggest how these individuals take responsibility for a community resources for a time. Technology stewarding adopts a community's perspective to help a community choose, configure and use technologies to best suit its needs. Tech stewards attend both to what happens spontaneously and what can happen purposefully, by plan and by cultivation of insights into what actually actually works" (p.24). How we perform this function will become clear later in the chapter.

Figure 1 presents a synthesis of Del's vision of the future of education. To explain in more concrete terms how we try to contribute to making this future come true, it is necessary to give some details about our status in Argentina as an educational project, especially because Del shares the basic characteristics mentioned above with other communities of the same kind, but can be said to depart from the usual features of a VCoP because of some reasons that will become clear in the following paragraphs.

Del is an *extension project,* a kind of educational initiative which is traditional in Argentinian universities and which is currently defined by the UNLP as a planning tool through which the knowledge and experience of all staff members (i.e., not only faculty members), and the students and graduates of any university share with the community their efforts to transform society and

Figure 1. The future of education, according to Del, as a word cloud.

culture, to disseminate knowledge and develop technology and the community in ways that allow society to improve its standard of living (UNLP, 2018). In practice, an extension project allows for the least traditional educational activities and, therefore, promotes innovation, variety and a positive outlook for what we believe education should become. Therefore we found this format an apt tool to enable the departure from mainstream, formal education which we expected to achieve with our VCoP (Enríquez, 2018).

At present, Del is managed by a group of 19 teachers, students and graduates of the UNLP, a state-owned university[2]. Extension projects in our university are always a dependency of the School its director belongs to. Because of this, Del belongs to the Facultad de Humanidades y Ciencias de la Educación (School of Humanities and Education Sciences, FaHCE), which offers five-year teacher education courses in over 20 disciplines. In fact, most of its members conduct studies in the field of education or have already finished degree and/or post-degree studies in this field.

In the first years of our activity, our main function was that of complementing the professional development program that Argentinian

---

2   Most major Argentinian universities are state-run and do not charge any kind of tuition to undergraduates, while the fees for post-degree studies tend to be low. This is due to the fact that the Argentinian educational system has a clearly social outlook which prioritizes the basic human right to education for all citizens.

teachers had access to in their own workplaces, or the post-degree courses that the Ministry of Education and other public institutions offered. Yet, in the last few years, and due to changes in national education policies, many of those opportunities have disappeared, and this has given a new significance to our project, which at present helps replace the previous offer. Even though this lack of clear policies for teacher formation cannot be welcome, it may have a positive side: the partial void it creates may give rise to alternative initiatives that push the boundaries of traditional education and help create new tendencies. At a time when the existence of the Internet cannot but facilitate this process, Del, like several other manifestations of the existence of entrepreneurial minds, provides an opportunity to try out, shape and reshape what may well become future learning tools for all kinds of learners. We hope that our work can be a realization of the fact that "everything 'revolutionary' taking place in learning has already happened at different scales, in bits and pieces, at different places," because we think we have already put into practice the idea that "The full impacts for ourselves and our organizations will be realized when we develop the courage to learn from each other's experiences and accept the risk and responsibility in applying a futures orientation in our praxis" (Moravec et al., 2015).

Part of the community leaders at Del, including all the authors of this chapter, are also members of an ongoing research project which belongs to the Instituto de Investigación en Humanidades y Ciencias Sociales, (Humanities and Social Sciences Research Institute, IdIHCS), a joint dependency of the FaHCE and the Consejo Nacional de Investigaciones Científicas y Técnicas (National Scientific and Technical Research Council, CONICET). Our project is meant to explore the ways and the extent to which knowledge is generated in VCoPs by studying the activity in Del, our own VCoP, and to observe how it can contribute to self- and peer-assisted learning beyond formal education institutions through the co-construction of new knowledge. Considering that Del has approximately 18,000 members, and about 10,000 visits per month, we also analyze if it is possible to perform our activity successfully with a high number of participants whose exchanges take place almost exclusively online.

The experience gained in these two projects forms the basis for our conclusions, and it has shown that teachers cannot become agents of change until they themselves have changed as learners.

Del was founded with the purpose of aiding teachers, teachers in training, and researchers in finding meaningful ways of incorporating technology into their professional and learning activities, following the premise that this use only makes sense when it adds new possibilities to teaching practices, or improves them. In other words, we have been convinced from the beginning that what matters most about new technologies is to understand how they can have a positive impact on learning (Moravec et al., 2015) This is why we have never followed the already dated tendency to equate the ability to incorporate technology in our teaching practice with only learning how to use digital tools and apps, but have focused on developing teaching methods and theory. In this sense, we fully endorse and have always put into practice the idea that "the network is the learning" (Siemens, 2007) and that, therefore, "Our traversals across networks are our pathways to learning, and as the network expands, so does our learning." (Moravec et al., 2015).

We believe that CoPs, whether virtual or offline, can help transform the future of education in several ways which are closely connected with the principles of Manifesto 15 (Moravec et al., 2015), which is also included as an appendix in this volume . There are two main reasons why we think so. First, CoPs can provide an opportunity for professionals and workers to acquire new knowledge through situated and informal learning. Second, teachers who learn in this kind of environment are more likely to become "nerds, geeks, makers, dreamers, and knowmads" who will help "build cultures of trust in our schools and communities" (Moravec et al., 2015) and find new ways of teaching their students how to learn outside, or besides, if need be, traditional and institutionalized methods.

What we will describe below shows that for the last five years we have been breaking some rules, both clearly understanding why we do so and, recently, also analysing our own performance in doing so. It also shows that we do not see technology as an answer (Moravec et al., 2015), but as a tool that provides opportunities to give new answers if we pose the right questions.

A VCoP in an educational institution?

Following Enríquez (2018), it is important to note that both CoPs and VCoPs are, in principle, generated and managed by peers rather than being created by an educational institution, which implies the need to follow its regulations besides creating their own and modifying them when necessary. Yet Del, which has this kind of institutional origin, has always been recognised as a VCoP by the board in charge of the evaluation of extension projects at the UNLP, as well as by other experts. We also consider ourselves a genuine VCoP, for the reasons that will become clear in the next paragraphs. Table 1 illustrates some ways in which, according to the same author, Del (a project which we might call an institutional VCoP) differs from communities organised by groups of professionals.

Gray (2004) argues that it is possible for VCoPs to develop a common identity by means of digital tools, and that this allows people with unusual or emerging practices to find a space where both experienced and beginning practitioners form their individual and collective identity. The knowledge produced in this way is based on expertise and is social, taking place in the way described by Siemens (2007) in connectivism. Therefore, we need to concentrate our efforts on helping individuals to make use of these resources and to create their own learning paths as they help others by sharing their personal knowledge and experience (see esp. Moravec et al., 2015).

How Del's members exchange and co-construct knowledge

Our institutional website is the starting point of our activity. It includes information about the nature of our project and a section called "Brújula" (compass), which shows the different paths members can follow to participate in our exchanges according to their specific interests and needs.

This website also contains a *Biblio- and Webgraphy*, which has a collection of links to different documents and websites related to the use of ICT in teaching and learning. Its contents range from the methodological, didactic and theoretical framework which supports the use of ICT in education to information about available digital tools and concrete experiences of their use

Table 1. Del's vision.

Like other CoPs...	Unlike other CoPs...
Del was created by a group of professionals belonging to an institution with common interests.	Del is an extension project that belongs to the administrative structure of a university.
A CoP is a disorganised, horizontal organisation.	The leading group can only be made up of staff members and students of the UNLP, and some of them form the institutional directing staff. The rest of the participants are freelance or belong to any other educational institution around the world.
We exchange professional knowledge (expertise, practice) and experiences.	The leading group is in charge of the knowledge stewarding and of reaching the objectives proposed in the project that the University has approved.
Our activity is occasionally complemented by a limited offer of formal courses.	These developments and/or post-degree courses are offered by a university which also issues the usual certificates of course attendance/completion.

in the classroom. This collection is constructed daily with the suggestions and links sent by members of the community.

We also have an institutional blog called *Didáctica y TIC*, besides different social networks which are used to share our publications and news, such as Facebook, Twitter (@linea_docentes), Instagram, LinkedIn, Google+, Scoop.it, and Red de Docentes de Iberoamérica OEI. We also share our contents and publications on Slideshare, RedDOLAC (Red de Docentes de América Latina y el Caribe), ResearchGate, and Academia.edu.

When we began our activity in 2013 we found that, in spite of our efforts to explain the way in which it was possible to exchange knowledge in our spaces, the notion of CoP was a novelty to many of those interested in joining us and their comments made it clear that they needed more details about how to participate. Our initial response was to offer a brief online course about CoPs, and to continue to listen to the members' needs and interests. Thus, to encourage participation, we decided to organize our activity around one central topic each month, through the publication of articles in our blog written by the community leaders or other invited specialists. We called it "Tema del mes" (Topic of the month) and encouraged members to leave comments or contributions about it. This, we thought, would make it easier for new members to understand how to learn from other members and to share their own expertise with the rest of the community. We have also invited specialists for interviews since August 2017 and have published these interviews in a new section of our blog, which we called "Entrevistas" ("Interviews").

Our expectation when we decided on the use of these spaces was to publish contents in our blog and to use social networks mainly to invite their users to take part in the debates in our institutional spaces but, as it is usual in these kinds of communities, the interests and preferences of the members led us in a different direction. The majority of them began to post comments in our social networks, and this motivated the inclusion of some new ones, the most recent of which is Instagram.

Each user has the same rights and possibilities to open a new debate or suggest another way of thinking, thus breaking down any possible hierarchical barrier. As real *knowmads*, they feel motivated to start or expand conversations and share information, moving smoothly as natural networkers. The leading team monitors these debates and intervenes to ensure that all exchanges follow netiquette.

This natural flux of ongoing conversations show us the way to organize future topics, always by following the lead of the needs and interests of our members because that is the nature of CoPs and, more than that, because we consider that this flexibility and adaptability are what ensures their efficacy of CoPs and makes them meaningful. We fully endorse the idea that the education of the future must leave behind the stagnation and adherence to old habits that has put it in such a need of change today. We are also convinced that a freer, more learner-oriented way of learning will help us realise the idea that it is necessary to encourage learners to be creative and innovative, so that they make a positive impact on the lives of all human beings (Moravec et al., 2015) In the meantime, while there is no other option for most learners than to continue attending more or less traditional schools, an initiative like ours can help to encourage innovation and evolution in teachers, which is an excellent first step to help learners gain the same habits.

As already noted, our sites receive around 10,000 visits per month, which represents a much higher number of participants than some theorists would find advisable. Yet, our practice and the amount of information we have been able to analyze in the first year of our research project show a sustained activity that seems to demonstrate that our work does bear its fruits. Our working hypothesis is that this co-construction of new knowledge takes place because Del breaks down into smaller "sub communities" in each of our social networks, as all of them have a relatively stable number of members who organize debates and exchanges among themselves, while others do the same in parallel on the other spaces of our VCoP. Even if these subgroups are still numerous, the fact that they represent only a fraction of the community makes the number of participants in each exchange much more acceptable.

The members of Del, just as any other Internet users, make use of the possibilities offered by Web 2.0 and generate new ways of learning by creating a VCoP that meets our interests and lies within our possibilities. So it is true for our community that "We cannot manage knowledge [...] *Knowledge* is about taking information and creating meaning at a personal level. We *innovate* when we take action with what we know to create new value" (Moravec et al., 2015).

In this sense, as our work philosophy fosters a hands-on kind of activity that allows the development of individual entrepreneurial skills, we believe that we have been providing a way for many teachers, students, and researchers to experience the truth in the idea that "The thrill of jumping off a cliff by deciding to do so yourself is a high you will never have if someone else pushes you off of it" (Moravec et al., 2015).

All the above describes the many ways in which our activity is that of a VCoP, and the fact we belong to a University and must follow its regulations makes us one of the possible kinds of genuine online communities. In addition, since the first days of our existence, many professionals and students have participated in our activities because they consider that the fact we belong to the UNLP guarantees the quality of our project. This appreciation of a traditional educational institution seems to contradict the general spirit of Manifesto 15, but even if this is so, it is a reality which has to be considered at present.

This community is, in our opinion, our individual realization of the fact that the future has already arrived, and our attempt to distribute it more evenly by making the fruit of our efforts accessible to all Internet users, since all our publications are open access.

Glocal transdisciplinary audiences: *knowmad* audiences?

Along its life, Del has reached multiple and diverse audiences that have given life to a community imbued with multicultural, multidisciplinary, local and global traits. An interesting view from which to consider these traits and the relations and tensions between local and global issues within the VCoP, as suggested by Gargiulo and Gómez (2018), is that presented by British sociologist Roland Robertson, who coined the concept of *glocalization* in an attempt to connect time-and-space discussions with universalism-and-particularism theories (Robertson, 1995). Robertson argues that "While globalization per se refers to a temporal process, glocalization injects a spatial dimension in its emphasis upon the *necessarily* spatial distribution of that which is being globalized..." (Robertson and White, 2005, p. 354).

Gargiulo and Gómez state that the nature of the transactions, interactions and knowledge generation within Del should be understood in the light of this powerful concept of glocalization, as the community members are scattered all over the world, and communication and knowledge creation take place both in synchronous and asynchronous ways, stretching over variable time intervals, long and short (cyber)spatial distances, as well as across academic and professional disciplinary boundaries and beyond. All of these glocal collaborative phenomena happen within the VCoP thanks to the generous, free contributions of Del's members; Furthermore, they are phenomena that rest on a glocal culture of mutual trust which the community leaders have been developing right since the origin of this community in 2013. This mutual trust implies acceptance and appreciation of *the other*, whether they are an intra- or an external-leading-team other, a same-discipline or a different-discipline *other*. It also requires a great deal of tolerance, open-mindedness and divergent thinking, to see learning and teaching practices through the eyes of *glocal others*, and enable co-thinking and co-creation to exist.

The fact that individuals from different cultural backgrounds, generations, and levels of expertise from various fields converge in our community enriches its activities and makes it grow and move forward along new paths. During these years, our websites and social networks have received visits from more than 118 countries, our main audience being from Mexico (25.99%) in the first place, followed by Argentina (24.69%) and the USA (11.87%), which shows that Del's audiences are not restricted to language or geographical boundaries.

All of Del's sites are only in Spanish, a fact which we thought would cause other glocal audiences who cannot communicate in Spanish to be excluded. Nevertheless, the third main group in Del's audience members belongs to a non-Spanish-speaking country, and we also have participants from many other non-Spanish-speaking countries. This means that we still reach non-Spanish-speaking audiences in countries where the existence of a language barrier could be expected. Rather than a problem, then, this is a good example of how our community has reached a wider variety of audiences than expected, and of how learning takes place informally online. Analysis of our website traffic using Google Analytics data shows that we have a global reach, spanning all six populated continents.

The concepts discussed in this section, and even our Google Analytics data, are, we think, relevant to an idea that is not explicit in Manifesto 15 but seems to hover over all its principles: those people, those we who are urged to take action and produce an 'innovution,' are all of us, inhabitants of the world, regardless of our country of origin and relationship to education. We feel the activity in Del is proof of what can be achieved in this sense; in fact, when our project began its public life, we expected to have a largely local, national audience but, in a matter of only hours, we had already received a larger and more varied number of contributions than we could have dreamt of, and they already came from different countries. This has shown us that all that is needed to facilitate change is to communicate our intentions to whoever wants to hear, and the collaboration, social learning and co-construction will come by themselves. This means that there is a yearning in all of us, people who are interested in education (we are deliberately not using the word 'specialists'), to act and produce change, which we will discuss in the next section.

Why do people come to our community?

It is clear that many educators feel the need to continue learning for different reasons: out of curiosity, as an obligation, for pleasure or simply for *themselves*. As Rexach (2017, p. 158) affirms, we can find three main categories of educational spaces for teachers in order to "solve the problem" of ICT in education: those focused on instrumental education, the ones based on the use of digital tools to complement or enrich the teaching and learning process, and last (and least frequently found), the ones that focus on soft skills[3] .

Some users come to our VCoP looking for a solution to an instrumental conception of technology. Indeed, experience has shown along these years that they gradually move on to the next step, understanding that an ofimatic kind of instruction (the basic office workers' tools) is not enough to face 21st-century classrooms.

When a teacher begins to engage in virtual environments, they have to perform basic actions such as accessing a website, looking for information, downloading files, learning to use software, sharing a link, participating in a forum discussion, and eventually writing collaboratively with their peers. These actions are not mere routines or technicalities, "... [t]hey have a tinge of the participation of a culture, they are a precursor to digital literacy, perhaps" (Rexach, 2017, p.164)[4]. Our work in Del aims at demonstrating that the experience of participating in a virtual learning environment clarifies the

---

3   Soft skills refer to a broad set of skills, competencies, behaviors, attitudes, and personal qualities that enable people to effectively navigate their environment, work well with others, perform well, and achieve their goals. These skills are broadly applicable and complement other skills such as technical, vocational, and academic skills. (Lippman et al., 2015, p.4).
4   Translation is ours.

meaning of the use of technology for educational purposes and makes it clear to teachers that it is not a question of introducing any kind of technology, but that it only makes sense to use those tools which provide a better alternative to traditional ones.

This approach to the way in which we view technology for education is based on the notion of *"tecnologías del aprendizaje y del conocimiento"*, also known as *"tecnologías para el aprendizaje y el conocimiento* (TAC)"[5], which refers to a use of technology that goes beyond merely learning to use ICT and aims at exploring these digital tools for learning and knowledge acquisition (Lozano, 2011). "TAC are those technological tools that we use to study, learn, gain or share knowledge. This pedagogical use of ICT implies moving from 'learning about technology' to 'learning *with* technology'" (Scorians, 2016, p.18)[6]. This shift, we believe, guarantees meaningful learning, as opposed to the kind of instrumental knowledge one can gain by using digital tools at random, without any purpose, or simply because they are in fashion. In other words, our answer to the question in principle 6 of Manifesto 15 is that technology may, at least in some cases, be the answer to how to improve the quality of teaching and learning. Yet, only time will tell if and how this may happen, because both the future of education and of the role of technology in it are being discussed at the moment, while we repeatedly try out, modify and sometimes discard or leave behind theories and practices that the constant evolution in this field presents us with.

We use technological tools to achieve specific goals but, at the same time, technology modifies our environment, our culture, our values, our habits and our social relationships (Burbules, 2001, p. 8) and, of course, our classrooms and the way we teach and learn. That explains the interest that these topics arouse, our hunger for more and, thus, the consistent growth of our community. Its members become *entreprenerds* (Moravec et al., 2015). They find in our community a living space to build knowledge collaboratively and, at the same time, build their learning paths individually, following their own interests and motivations. This is a key factor to achieve not only individual goals but also to keep the community alive. It is this plurality that keeps pushing the horizon line further and further, building bridges beyond our expectations.

---

5   Learning and knowledge technologies, also knowns as technologies for learning and knowledge.
6   Translation is ours.

In this regard, because we see it in practice, we adhere to J. Lave's view (1991), when she proposes to "consider learning not as a process of socially shared cognition that results in the end in the internalization of knowledge by individuals, but as a process of becoming a member of a sustained community of practice. Developing an identity as a member of a community and becoming knowledgeably skillful are part of the same process, with the former motivating, shaping, and giving meaning to the latter, which it subsumes" (p. 65). The "*El futuro de la educación (en nuestras manos)*" conference, organized by Del's leading team and held in the FaHCE, in 2016, provides a good example of what this kind of activity can bring about.

Present and future of Del's journey

Looking at what our community has done so far and at what we expect to be able to do in the future gives us a sense of achievement but, also, urges us to move forward and to continue to participate in the inspiring adventure of collaborating in building the future of education, a privilege that former generations did not have. Our success to date shows that we have been able to construct the following:

- Del provides its members with the possibility of enabling asynchronous and, on occasion, synchronous collaboration with individuals from diverse age groups, cultural backgrounds and levels of expertise, individuals who have come to acquire various teaching and learning practices.
- The fact that it is a VCoP, on the other hand, can make this community reach more individuals worldwide, even those who live and work in more remote and less favored areas.
- This communal sharing facilitates the worldwide dissemination and circulation of common topics of interest for the members of the community and, at the same time, encourages the interconnected aspect of knowledge building: the glocal network is the learning. Del's members possess glocal cultural identities and have had diverse digital experiences; these two facts stimulate reflection and thinking about self-backgrounds in the light of the other members' backgrounds.

- Working as part of a VCoP might well help its members develop and/or enhance communication skills and their intra- and intercultural competence since the very nature of communal life rests on words and images used to exchange effectively and build knowledge almost exclusively on an online physical stratum. This, which is only a hypothesis at the moment, is part of the analysis we are carrying out in our current research project.
- We see our VCoP as a training space, a sandbox where members can learn and teach themselves by doing, through experiential learning.
- We believe that a VCoP like Del is a sample of a collaborative initiative to co-create new education futures. We consider that Del is a knowmad community inside our present-day knowmad society: a group of individuals following the same interests, each of them valued for their personal knowledge, working collaboratively in a non-hierarchical way and led by innovation and co-creation. Individuals who understand that knowledge is socially constructed (and, as Lave (1991) says, much more than a process which is merely socially shared), consider learning a lifelong process and feel "responsible for designing their own futures" (Moravec, 2013, p. 19).

Our future will very probably find us looking for new and better tools to continue to tackle some challenges which arise from our diversity and ever changing activity:

- Along the years, the inclusion of new members coming from diverse fields of knowledge has posed the challenge for the leading team of developing the strategies and skills needed to carry out our teamwork collaboratively and harmoniously. This has been a demanding task, given the fact that we have formed a group of individuals whose scholarly knowledge has ranged from the so-called *soft sciences*, for example, modern languages, psychology, journalism and educational sciences to the so-called hard sciences, such as astronomy, mathematics and computer science, that is, individuals whose cognitive styles have been pressed and shaped by the particular learning mode of each field of studies along their training paths and academic careers.

- We can say something similar about the diversity of the disciplines taught and studied by the rest of the members, who also come from all educational levels, from kindergarten to university degree and post-degree teachers. This adds to the complexity of the relationships in the community and of the possibilities of shared knowledge building and has to be taken into account by the leading team at the time of selecting topics and approaches to them. Our policy has usually been to deal with every topic in such a way that those who have no previous knowledge of it can understand it, but complementing it with information or reading materials for those who want to enlarge their knowledge of a topic they have visited before.

The original plan for Del, submitted to the UNLP in 2012, drew interesting and innovative ideas from several theories and studies which were recent then and are still valid now in most cases. To our (pleasant) surprise, a few years later Manifesto 15 appeared to summarise what the authors of initiatives like ours thought and were trying to put into practice. This is why, in this chapter, we have set out to show in what ways our activity contributes to the realisation of its principles and is helping to bring about the changes that are necessary for the future of education. In fact, we think that all CoPs and VCoPs can, like ours, provide an opportunity for the more creative, informal and continuous forms of learning that are necessary to begin to change education in the present and project it into the future. Circumstances have placed us in the world at the right place and time to have the opportunity to participate in this serious enterprise which, at the same time, often feels like a playground in which we can "dream, create, make, explore, learn and promote entrepreneurial, cultural, or social endeavors, taking risks and enjoying the process as much as the final outcome, without fearing the potential failures or mistakes that the journey includes." (Moravec et al., 2015), because we feel (and, in fact, are) so free to follow our best instinct. We do not forget that we are supported by one of those traditional educational institutions that we are trying to reshape, and that makes us smile and gives us hope.

REFERENCES

Burbules, N. and Callister, T. (2001). *Educación: Riesgos y promesas de las nuevas tecnologías de la información*. Buenos Aires: Granica.

Dale, S. (2009). Communities of practice: Turning conversations into collaboration. es.slideshare. net/stephendale/cop-conversations-to-collaboration-presentation

Docentes en línea. (2016, April 30). *El futuro de la educación (en nuestras manos)* conference. Facultad de Humanidades y Ciencias de la Educación, UNLP. blogs.unlp.edu.ar/didacticaytic/la-educacion-del-futuro-el-futuro-ya-esta-aqui/

Enríquez, S. (2018). Herramientas para una comunidad virtual de práctica. Manuscript submitted for publication. Proceedings from the *III Congreso Internacional Humanidades Digitales*. Rosario, Argentina.

Gargiulo, S., and Gómez, M. (2018). La comunidad de práctica virtual DeL: Puente(s) entre audiencias globales multiculturales y multidisciplinares. Manuscript submitted for publication. Proceedings from the *III Congreso Internacional Humanidades Digitales*. Rosario, Argentina. La cultura de los datos.

Gray, B. (2004). Informal learning in an online community of practice. *Journal of Distance Education/ Revue de l'enseignement à distance, 19*(1), 20–35.

Lave, J. (1991). Situating learning in communities of practice. In Resnick, L. B., Levine, J. M., & Teasley, S. D. (Eds.), *Perspectives on socially shared cognition* (pp. 63-82). Washington, DC: American Psychological Association.

Lave, J and Wenger, E. (1991). *Situated learning: Legitimate peripheral participation*. Cambridge: Cambridge University Press.

Lippman, L., Ryberg, R., Carney, R., & Moore, K. (2015). *Workforce connections. Key "soft skills" that foster youth workforce success: Toward a consensus across fields*. Bethesda, MD: Child Trend Publications.

Lozano, R. (2011). Las 'TIC/ TAC': De las tecnologías de la información y comunicación a las tecnologías del aprendizaje y del conocimiento. dialnet.unirioja.es/ servlet/articulo?codigo=3647371

Moravec, J.W. (Ed.). (2013). *Knowmad Society*. Minneapolis: Education Futures.

Moravec, J.W. et al. (2015). *Manifesto 15*. Minneapolis: Education Futures. manifesto15.org

100 Emerging education futures

Rexach, V. (2017). Aprender para enseñar mejor. Formación docente en tiempos de tecnologías digitales. In Montes, N. (Ed.), *Educación y TIC. De las políticas a las aulas* (pp. 157-183). Buenos Aires: Eudeba.

Robertson, R. (1995). Glocalization: Time-space and homogeneity-heterogeneity. In Featherstone, M., Lash, S., and Robertson, R., *Global Modernities* (pp. 25-44). London: Sage Publications.

Robertson, R., & White, K.E. (2005). Globalization: Sociology and cross-disciplinarity. In Calhoun, C., Rojek, K., & Turner, B. (Eds.), *The Sage Handbook of Sociology* (pp. 345-366). London: Sage Publications.

Scorians, E.E. (2016). *Propuesta de capacitación en escritura en inglés para alumnos de Geofísica de la Facultad de Ciencias Astronómicas y Geofísicas (UNLP) a través de la implementación de TAC* (Doctoral dissertation). www.memoria.fahce.unlp.edu.ar/tesis/te.1355/te.1355.pdf

Siemens, G. (2007). The network is the learning. www.youtube.com/watch?v=rpbkdeyFxZw

Universidad Nacional de La Plata. (2018). *Bases para la convocatoria de proyectos para centros comunitarios de extensión universitaria*. La Plata, Argentina: UNLP.

Wenger-Trayner, E., & Wenger-Trayner, B. (2015). Introduction to communities of practice: A brief overview of the concept and its uses. wenger-trayner.com/introduction-to-communities-of-practice/

Wenger, E., White, N., & Smith, J.D. (2009). *Digital habitats: Stewarding technology for communities*. Portland, OR: CPsquare.

Silvia C. Enríquez works at the Facultad de Humanidades y Ciencias de la Educación, Universidad Nacional de La Plata as an adjunct professor of english language, director of Docentes en línea, and of an associated research project. She is coordinator of the special courses at the School of Languages. s.enriquez@fahce.unlp.edu.ar

Sandra Beatriz Gargiulo is a sworn translator from UNLP, and a translator trainer at Tecnicatura Superior en Traducción Técnica y Científica en Lengua Inglesa, Ministry of Security, Buenos Aires, Argentina. She works as a freelance translator, and for Universidad Nacional de La Plata as a teacher. sbgargiulo@gmail.com

María J. Ponz is a master's degree student specializing in information technology applied to education at Facultad de Informática, Universidad Nacional de La Plata. She is a coordinator of Docentes en línea. She teaches English at Colegio Bosque del Plata and the School of Languages at UNLP. mariajimenaponz@gmail.com

Erica E. Scorians works at the Facultad de Humanidades y Ciencias de la Educación, Universidad Nacional de La Plata as an assistant teacher of introduction to the English language. She is a coordinator of Docentes en línea, and is also a freelance English-Spanish translator and teacher. escorians@gmail.com

NOTES

Notes

Notes

Notes

It's all in the approach: Transforming education for all

ROBERT THORN

The best way forward:
The elusive paradigm shift

Among the myriad reform proposals, best practice lists, revolutionary new systems, technology marvels, often out of the reach of teachers around the world, there is a way forward, that is accessible to all communities and can be used in transforming education now. We at Developing Real Learners (DRL), and an increasing number of organisations (Claxton, 2018, p. 6), are turning to and promoting a different approach to education. This approach is at once fundamental, immediate, and both culturally, and socially inclusive. It is transformative because it comes from the heart of what it means to be human. This chapter describes the evolution of an *approach framework* that schools can apply to bring sustainable, affordable transformation[7] almost immediately.

Of the many ways forward for education, I believe that a change in our approach is needed before any other reform, revolution, or other reshuffling can truly bring the results we need schools to provide. Like the proverbial doctor curing the symptoms rather than identifying the cause, so many changes in education seem to not live up to expectations. Some fail to be culturally transferrable (Fuhrmann & Beckmann-Dierkes, 2011) others are out of reach of those who cannot afford them. All of them do not really get to the heart of the matter.

Within us lies great potential—we are born learners[8] and remain learners all our lives and yet our natural characteristics as learners are often suppressed, neglected, or damaged in the process of school and especially in secondary school (Land, 2011).

I argue, like many, that we should be providing young people with what they really need to become successful. In place of being the best students they can be, we set objectives to a higher level—to be the best holistic learners they can be. If you work in a school with young people, you can ask them or your colleagues a few questions: What is the point of school? What makes a good school? What are the attributes (the habits, skills and dispositions) of people who are good at learning through life? Do we help young people develop these in our school?

In my experiences at many schools in various countries, I asked the questions posed above, always to secondary schoolers (age 11-18) and often

---

7   I use the term *transformation* to mean inclusive and gradual change – not replacing things but changing the perspective of what is there. I use 'transformation' in place of reform (moving the same things around to improve results following the same perspective) and revolution (where change happens suddenly, and people get hurt one way or another).
8   Here I use the term *learners* to stand for *holistic learners* and in place of the word *students*. This is to keep in mind that we are developing learners for life rather than just learners for school.

to teachers and parents. The reactions to such questions, asked in a coaching manner, reveal the fundamental flaw in the mainstream approach to education I have found exists so often not only in state schools around the world but in progressive private schools too.

Putting these questions and reactions together creates what I call an *approach framework*: a sequence of questions and guidelines that forms a structure that the school community responds to. The framework questions are sustained apart from slight deviations in translation, but the answers are determined by the school community members and depend on their cultural references and perspectives.

So, the following takes us through such an approach framework...

Asking the right questions

Having read and been inspired by Professor Guy Claxton's 'What's the Point of School?' (Claxton, 2008), I would ask people that question. It always led to interesting answers, such as:

- To educate our children;
- To give young people the best start in life;
- To make sure our children have the qualifications to be employable; and,
- So, they have good opportunities and choices later in life.

These are all genuine concerns of teachers, parents and the young people themselves. The problem was that these very valid answers were in fact being interpreted in very different ways. It depends on our view of what education is in how we interpret the first response in the list. To some, the best start in life may be a piece of paper allowing you into higher education irrespective of being able to cope with university. The best start in life might be viewed by one person as having the qualifications to go to the next level while for another it might be how developed you are as a global citizen. One person's view of what's needed to be employable might be set by their own out-of-date experience, whereas the truth is that things have moved on and employers look for other factors. It depends on what opportunities you are thinking about whether you encourage young people to take a traditional route to being members of the traditional professions (i.e., doctor, lawyer, or engineer) or to allow them to become online entrepreneurs, gamers, or entering the traditional professions with a growth-mindset, which will attract the best partner in your community? Which leads to your happier of more successful?

I began to ask slightly different questions:

What do young people really need from education?
What should schools be doing for young people?

And this immediately led to:

How can schools provide that?

These questions get us to the heart of the matter. I believe if we can answer these two questions, we can move schools forward.

In one role, I worked with just over one hundred secondary learners aged between eleven to eighteen over a period of several months. The aim was to have these learners go through a process towards answering the second of the three questions above.

With the help of their teachers, we set the scene by getting the kids, in their individual classes, to think about and discuss the best sort of environment one might want in a school. We introduced some ideas from Peter Senge's work on schools as learning organisations (Senge et al., 2012). We discussed the need for *trust* within a community and for effective and sensitive *communication* and for *collaboration* bringing us to a point where we might be able to agree on a way forward and derive a shared vision. Gradually, learners and teachers became used to answering some tough questions about themselves and their community together. After several weeks of this exploration, learners were ready to answer important questions without feeling they needed to 'provide the right answer' or try to 'guess what was in the teacher's head' or feel they had nothing to say.

Having been through this process, we then put classes together and asked the first of our two main questions:

What should school be doing for young people?

After several weeks of structured debate, research, argument, collaboration, and the making of new friendships and new understandings, the emergent response was: *Schools should maximise the opportunities for young people to be happy and successful in the future.*

The students still had the idea that education was primarily for a 'future' that was quite a distant thing for many of them. We discussed the 'future' and kids agreed that they didn't just want to be happy and successful in the future but could have some of that right now. So, they edited their final group reply to become: *Schools should maximise the opportunities for young people to be happy and successful now and in the future.*

Along the way, they debated what *happiness* really meant to them, and even the less mature pupils recognised and agreed that there were different modes of happiness. One older learner pointed out that the things we do to be happy is like the food we eat: some types of food satisfy us, while others do not, and some even make us ill. "What we say makes us happy—you know, games and all that—isn't always the thing that really satisfies us" (Grade 11 girl, 2017). After discussion, the majority of kids agreed that happiness comes from doing something constructive, usually for others, the environment, or for themselves. Through the school's service and action programme, through what their parents did with them, or through what kids had realised and done by themselves, they concluded constructive action led to a certain level of satisfaction and happiness.

Having defined happiness, they struggled a bit with *success* until someone came up with the idea that success was really being able to be happy most of the time. Finally, they decided that real success was all about maximising the chances of being happy and in making others happy. Some students included animals in this and some included *the planet*.

And then they would go off to maths, languages, and science classes and taught bits of things seemingly at random just in case they were useful. They went to classes that never touched on their happiness and told half-truths about a different sort of success, the one where they sacrifice their childhood in order for some to get a piece of paper, a diploma. This leads to our second question:

How can schools provide what young people really need?

How do we help young people maximise their chances of happiness and success now and in the future? I had the chance to run workshops for schools where I could ask teachers and school leaders, and sometimes parents, "what do young people really need for happiness and success?" The people I asked came from a wide range of cultures and backgrounds. I have found that they, quite amazingly, all pretty much come out with the same things: a mixture of skills and dispositions which sometimes emerge as habits and which have been collectively called "attributes" (IBLP, 2013). People from diverse cultures that I have engaged with in countries such as Mozambique, Japan, Switzerland, Turkey, Georgia, Qatar, Slovakia, Lebanon, Russia, Pakistan, Iran, and India, have identified the same or similar attributes that they feel are important for the success and happiness of young people. Why this is not odd is that, of course, they recognise the human qualities that underpin our well-being and therefore our success and happiness in a better world, a world which those young people can create by developing these attributes.

There have been many attempts to identify these attributes (Ritchhart, 2002, pp. 24-25), and those who are familiar with the International Baccalaureate's learner profile (International Baccalaureate Organization, 2013) will see that the language I've used to group the responses of all those people we asked is influenced by my previous work with that organisation. One major difference, however, is the ability of communities to add attributes that are important to them as long as they meet the criteria for an attribute.

Table 2. Examples of attributes of holistic learners.

Heart-mindedness	Communication	Collaboration
compassionate, empathetic, and caring enough to get to the heart of the matter	being able to communicate well and appropriately with others and oneself	being able to give one's best to the group and get the best out of others
Curious inquiry	**Anti-fragility**	**Jugaar/jugaad**
wanting to ask great questions and being able to find answers	always improving through active and growth-based reflection	having the innovative resourcefulness to make the best of what one has
Ways of thinking	**Balance**	**Growth-mindedness**
Being able to think in different ways as appropriate	seeking balance in one's life and in one's development	believing one can develop and manage one's learning attributes. Seeking to learn and improve as learners rather than blame when things go wrong
Being proactive	**Independence**	**Wise in risk-taking**
being able to take action and responsibility	Being able to learn and develop independently	being courageous enough to do the right thing and go outside your comfort zone)
Knowing and understanding	**Principled/open-mindedness**	**More?**
having a deep and wide-ranging knowledge you can use to be wise	expanding one's principles through open-mindedness; defining one's open-mindedness through one's principles	every community is different, perhaps you see other attributes that make great holistic learners?

Note. Jugaar/Jugaad is an Urdu/Hindi term describing 'innovation in the face of adversity' or 'doing more with less' (Radjou et al., 2012)

Table 2 displays attributes of holistic learners we have identified, gathering responses from people in schools in the above countries. It seems to me, these are also the attributes needed to develop entrepreneurial spirit. Importantly, they are the attributes needed to develop what I call *active wisdom*[9], not just being able to determine the best decisions, but having the capability to take action on those decisions to create positive change.

It is always interesting to see teachers' reactions when I ask, "Who here teaches these attributes?" Of course, all good teachers help young people develop these attributes to some extent. However, they also unwittingly do much to suppress, ignore, and damage their development through usual practices found in many schools (Thorn, 2018). The problem I have seen in the schools I have worked in as an educator, consultant, or coach is that the development of these attributes (which are not specifically or immediately possessing anything to do with studying at school, but are for learning and developing as a learner) are not explicitly developed in the schools and their development is very much left to chance.

Teachers need to be allowed to identify where they may develop these attributes and then explore what they can change about their practice in order to provide more opportunities for young people to develop them. They need to be helped to coach learners into becoming coaches themselves, and develop holistic learners who can identify and create their own opportunities for attribute development.

The question for the education community is then, "What can schools do to really help young people develop the attributes they need?"

Our organisation's burning question is: *How can we help all schools approach education so that everything they do (within whatever curriculum they use) coaches young people to focus on becoming the best holistic learners they can be, developing for life and therefore living a life devoted to the pursuit of, and participation with, active wisdom?*

---

9 In my institution, we view *active wisdom* as the culmination of the developed attributes; being able to manage oneself and others and make the right decisions and act on them

How schools can (and are) providing what young people really need

Ideally, the process I've developed for DRL starts with a period of exploration by the whole community: learners, teachers, and parents. The scene needs to be set, the environment of sharing ideas and critical friendship needs to be developed, and the process of looking deeper for answers needs to be recognised. This phase is important to undo the effects of an approach to education that relies on and develops compliance and "correct answer-giving" (Jackson & Zmuda, 2014). The old approach limits people's ability to see beyond the answers they feel are expected or those they have heard repeated. When asked, young people will often say that school is about learning things so they can "have an education," "get a good job in the future," or so they can "go to university." The shallowness of their answers is often due to the fact that they have heard the answers to a question they have never been encouraged to consider for themselves. By asking challenging questions such as, "What is the point of school?" and, "How can we transform our school into a learning community?" followed by facilitated discussion, young people, and indeed parents and teachers, gradually come to realise that education really ought to be for much more than teaching just-in-case information and a belief that school is only about working towards passing exams.

By engaging in discussion about what young people really need from school, communities can engage in identifying better outcomes that schools can provide. Such outcomes include helping youth develop into people who are really qualified and ready for now and the future. In my experience, through community discussion, in no matter which culture, what defines us as human gradually surfaces and the attributes of holistic learners emerge as the most important focus for education.

Learner-development-centred approaches to education.

Learner-development-centred (LDC) approaches are close to learner-centred approaches but go slightly further in helping the learner to develop themselves and others. Previous to learner-centred came student centred and teacher centred approaches thus making LDC approaches the latest in the evolutionary chain of educational approaches. An LDC approach is one in which the development of the attributes of holistic learners is the focus. The attributes are developed within contexts such as school subject areas, hobbies, everyday life). An LDC approach immediately gives young people a very clear reason for going to school and attending classes that previously seemed irrelevant – the classes are now the focus of self-development of attributes that help the learner to get the best out of themselves and others – to be successful and happy in their lives today. The goals of LDC approaches are to help young people become the best holistic learners they can be; to enable them to identify an create opportunities to develop themselves and others as holistic learners and to set the learner on the path to active wisdom and of becoming the best holistic learner one can be.

Developing real learners: Learner-development-centred (LDC) approaches to education.

Over the years, I have come to believe that, ideally, all members of the community should approach education with the intent to develop learner attributes. The development of habits, skills, and dispositions needs a context and the context most secondary schools have readily available and are familiar with are the wonderful subject areas traditionally studied. Many, primary schools already have the context of play, personal development, and project-based learning which lend themselves well to attribute development. However, where teaching is subject-based, the subject needs to be used as the context in which opportunities for learner development takes place. This ultimately involves teachers, and gradually learners themselves, identifying and creating opportunities for attribute development within the context of the subject areas that schools teach. By adopting such a strategic approach, any school may both help young people develop as holistic learners and also as 'students' who can pass courses with understanding. I believe that the more content-laden and prescribed a curriculum is, the more difficult it is to create opportunities within them for explicit attribute development, it is still possible to develop attributes in a determined community.

Learner-development-centred (LDC) education happens when we shift the paradigm from teaching subjects toward not just instructing them or even teaching children but actively coaching them (Aguilar, 2013). The coaching role that good teachers display is emphasised and developed. It is nurtured explicitly in the lives and development of learners as a means of developing a new purpose for a school based on personal development, the pursuit of the 'active wisdom' I mentioned above.

So, practically, how do we start with adopting an LDC approach? There are many ways to start this and each school will need to decide which way is best for them. Some will need a long introduction period of "setting the scene" and others will have a critical mass of ready community members almost immediately. The interesting thing we found is that, whether it is a few learners starting this or the school leadership team, intent on using the approach for themselves, or, as in our current case, a school intent on spreading the idea globally, there is an approach for each case. LDC approaches are ultimately flexible and adaptable.

One way to bring good results is to follow this process:
- First, one has to understand the need for change and the shift in paradigm. Engaging the community with the challenging questions of what young people really need and what schools should be doing for them can set the scene. It raises awareness that the school is open to different approaches, that new ideas are being called for, and that it is safe to say what one feels.
- Use preparatory discussion topics such as, "How are our levels of trust in our

community?", "Do we really communicate well with each other?", and, "Are we making the most out of our opportunities to collaborate?" as keys towards coming to a shared vision on creating a learning community that will be able to employ an LDC approach.

- Introduce questions such as, "what is the point of school?", "What should be the point of school?", and "What should education be providing young people?" to help arrive at the need for developing learner attributes.
- Explore and build an understanding of the attributes so that the community has a good idea of what everyone means by each attribute.
- Identify what is present in current practice that provides an opportunity for attribute development.
- Investigate which opportunities for attribute development[10] could be realised with easy changes to teaching and learning in school by individual teachers.
- Provide teachers with a challenge to collaborate to find ways to develop attributes in their classes and report back on progress and findings.
- Provide space and time for learners to identify ways they can develop the attributes in each lesson they attend, in their daily lives, and in their hobbies.
- Provide space and time for young people to identify what their teachers can do to help them with their attribute development and to create opportunities for them to develop while still learning the subjects the system wants them to learn.
- Hold events for teachers and learners to share ideas, view progress, and set goals for progression.
- Identify educators and learners in the community who can form the school's outreach team in order to introduce the ideas and processes to other schools in their area.

---

10 Here I don't mean tokenism. It is not enough for teachers to tell learners to "get into groups and solve this problem" and claim that his is developing collaborators. We have to use the opportunity that the context subject can be learnt in a group to develop strategies for the most appropriate forms of collaboration for the task and for ways to reflect such that learners learn about themselves and others such that they can collaborate better each time. The same can be said for all attributes. If identifying and creating opportunity for attribute development is the first pillar of an LDC approach, then explicitly developing each attribute seriously is the second.

- Set up local, regional, and international associations and connections in order to: A) learn through sharing ideas, progress, and cultures; B) help others learn from one's approaches, progress, and cultural interpretations; and, C) pave the way for changes in educational systems to make it easier for adoption and implementation of LDC approaches.

In this way, LDC approaches can be adopted, improve education and gradually help communities help their governments transform the system from the inside. This means improvement in education now, not waiting for government reform. It also supports the success of young people within the current system while providing good reason and direction for changes within it. An LDC approach involves the community and especially the learners taking control of the system and using it to the best advantage of both.

In using this framework, school communities allow themselves to take control of education, not of simply mass-producing students for future study or for jobs, but in developing holistic learners for a better community and for all life has to offer.

So, to recap the process in a different way, firstly, one has to perceive there's an issue with the way we're approaching education. Everyone involved needs to think about this. At least one person in the school community needs to raise concerns. It can be a school leader, but that doesn't have to be where it starts; it could be a teacher or a parent or, of course, a learner or a group of learners such as a student council or other interest group. Whoever it is, they will need to be quite persistent and patient. Not everyone will listen or want to hear. You are, after all, "rocking the boat" and there will be people who feel that the boat is best left steady.

Secondly, one needs to prepare one's school. Is your school ready for some tough questions around the levels of trust, communication, and collaboration between all members of the school community? Raising awareness and tackling outstanding issues where trust is lacking, communication is poor, or collaboration is weak to non-existent is key.

Next, comes alignment of the development of learner attributes alongside the learning of subjects. Teachers have to begin to use their subjects as contexts in which to provide opportunities for young people to develop as learners. Learners need to help them do this. As good teachers naturally develop at least some of the attributes to some extent, the process is to first identify what we do already, emphasise it, and make it explicit in our plans. Next, is to look at what we teach and identify what we can easily change to better provide opportunities for young people to develop learner attributes. After that, teachers need to look at where they are not providing young people the opportunities to develop and work on ways to change this.

LEARNERS NEED TO BE ENGAGED IN THE PARADIGM SHIFT IF IT IS TO WORK. THEY NEED TO BE GRADUALLY MADE AWARE OF THE CHANGE THE SCHOOL NEEDS TO GO THROUGH.

In the process, teachers will need to develop a deep understanding of the attributes and what those attributes mean to them and their community and engage in the above process. For example there are great debates to be had on the interaction between open-mindedness and being principled as a learner. There may be issues in discussing to what extent a learner should become independent and what collaboration really means. There may be questions on how heart-minded[11] society is around them, how it really should be, and how they really want it to be. All these discussions are healthy and vital. People will, of course, bring the wisdom of their cultures as well as the baggage they have been carrying around with them, and a time of uncertainty may emerge when there is a certain amount of unpacking and repacking done. I argue this process strengthens one's culture. If aspects of our culture cannot stand questioning, then those aspects are probably something we have forgotten the fundamental reason for and just do mindlessly. Questioning makes our cultures relevant, strong, and meaningful. With such an awareness of our cultures, our cultures also, in turn, makes us relevant, strong, and meaningful.

---

11 The term is used by DRL to pull together various aspects of someone who really cares: "Putting one's heart" into what one does; "Having a heart" and empathy for others and other life; caring enough to "get to the heart of the matter" and therefore being able to solve issues properly.

Parents, usually desperate for ways to support the emerging adults in their families, will be glad to find that in supporting the development of attributes, nagging is replaced by gentle coaching. This is something that young people will more easily recognise as caring than constant reprimanding. Sharing one's wisdom and life experience (even if it concerns what wasn't provided at school) becomes a resource for young people. Gentle coaching questions may lay the foundation for the development of the parent as well as for the child or adolescent just as this approach allows for teachers to find themselves and their purpose again through their work.

With the majority of educators, learners, and parents developing within a community of trust, effective communication, cultural sensitivity, and collaboration, a truly shared vision is able to emerge. With a shared vision of developing holistic learners within the contexts of subjects and out-of-class life, we are paving the way for the development of active wisdom, the culmination of the development of learner attributes. It is about knowing oneself and how to get the best out of oneself. It is about knowing how to help others get the best out of themselves. It is about knowing how to get the best out of one's culture and how to learn from others while recognising similarities and celebrating differences. It is not just about knowing the best things to do next; it is about taking action in doing what is best. If schools make the paradigm shift and move become learner-development-centred communities, perhaps they may just not only make their communities a better place but also the wider world with which they are connected.

What are the outcomes?

Immediate outcomes

By developing holistic learners several major changes happen in the community:

- Young people now have a reason for attending school, and for attending the classes they dislike. Those that love school have an additional, deeper reason for loving it. They are developing themselves to be good at what they are doing now (and in the future), and they are becoming more competent at life—happier and more successful.

- Teachers as coaches regain lost value. They are now appreciated as supporting coaches of learners, teasing the best out of kids rather than telling them what to do, and they get learners to decide what to do for themselves. With this value comes a sense of fulfilment. You are everyone's coach and you are a helping hand to each young person in aiding them to support themselves develop into the best of what they can be.
- Parents also have a chance to become the coaches of their youngsters. Rather than telling them to work harder, study more, and becoming frustrated in the process—and, on the other hand, rather than leaving them to their own devices to learn for themselves—suddenly, through LDC approaches, parents are guided towards becoming the people who can help youth reflect on their choices, make good decisions, and make mistakes in the safety of the parent's confidence. Because the primary goal is to set young people off on the path to wisdom (especially active wisdom) the relationship between adults and young people becomes one of nurturing learners rather than of forced relationships pushing students through a system that is, at best, partially useful to the young person and the society they live within.

Long-term objectives

At DRL, we are implementing the start of the transformation process towards an LDC approach in Slovakia with the following objectives:

- To share our framework with other schools, locally, leading to the development of a regional network;
- To collaborate on parallel implementation with partners who have shown an interest in several other regions, leading to an inter-regional network;
- To establish the principle of ensuring that learning communities are sharing communities;
- Introduce online, face-to-face and blended options for coaching and training school-based community coaches and catalysts, who will lead to the introduction of LDC approaches to the financially poorest of school communities; and,
- Help the emergence of a generation that can lead a more sustainable and compassionate civilisation.

REFERENCES

Aguilar, E. (2013). *The art of coaching: Effective strategies for school transformation.* San Francisco: Wiley.

Claxton, G. (2018). *The learning power approach: Teaching learners to teach themselves.* UK: Crownhouse.

Claxton. G. (2008). *What's the point of school?: Rediscovering the heart of education.* Oxford: Oneworld.

Fuhrmann, J., & Beckmann-Dierkes, N. (2011). Finland's PISA Success: Myth and transferability. *KAS International Reports 7.* www.kas.de/c/document_library/get_file?uuid=4e6fb94d-fab7-0b3e-ce46-27143c2238eb

International Baccalaureate Organization. (2013). The IB learner profile. www.www.ibo.org

Jackson, R., & Zmuda, A. (2014). 4 (secret) keys to student engagement, *Educational Leadership, 72*(1), 18–24.

Land, G. (2011). The Failure of Success. *TEDxTucson,* Tucson, AZ. www.youtube.com/watch?v=ZfKMq-rYtnc

Radjou, N., Prabhu, J., & Ahuja, S. (2012). *Jugaad innovation.* Gurgaon: Random House India.

Senge, P., Cambron-McCabe, N., Lucas, T., Smith, B., Dutton, J. and Kleiner, A. (2012). *Schools that learn.* London: Nicholas Brearly.

Taleb, N.N. (2012). *Antifragile: Things that gain from disorder.* London: Penguin.

Thorn, R. (2018). *The anti-learner attributes: Problems teacher don't know they have.* Unpublished manuscript.

Robert Thorn is Managing Director of the non-profit organization, Developing Real Learners, and head of secondary at The English International School of Bratislava in the Slovak Republic. robert.thorn@developingreallearners.org

Notes

notes

....

....

....

....

....

....

....

....

....

....

....

....

....

....

....

....

notes

A heutagogical approach to rheology

ERLING N. DAHL

EINAR N. STRØMMEN

TOR G. SYVERTSEN

Introduction

The college lecture is to Nobel Laureate Carl Wieman the educational equivalent of bloodletting, long overdue for revision (Westervelt, 2016). Nonetheless, many universities still pursue 'teaching quality' by fervently trying to improve the obscure quality of classroom lectures, with no regard to learning. Learning requires mental activity in the learner's mind and implies changes in the learner's brain. Lecturing, on the other hand, as George Leonard purportedly noted, "is the best way to get information from teacher's notebook to student's notebook without touching the student's mind."

John Archibald Wheeler remarked: "We all know that the real reason universities have students is in order to educate the professors" (Christensen, 2009). This is what every teacher has always known; you learn most by teaching. This insight was established two millennia ago by Seneca the younger's *Docendo discimus*, "by teaching, we learn" ("Docendo Discimus", n.d.).

This simple principle is applied in the 'Feynman Technique,' named after the Nobel Laureate physicist Richard P. Feynman (Farnam Street, 2012). Every teacher should facilitate learning for her/his students and for the self, rather than focusing on her/his own teaching performance.

Still, pedagogy is a major issue among university administrators. The term stems from Greek paidagogos, a slave who escorted boys to school and supervises them, hence education of children. University students are adults, and the proper term for adult education is *andragogy* (andr- meaning 'man' and agogos meaning 'leader of').

Stewart Hase and Chris Kenyon coined the term heutagogy for self-driven learning (Hase & Kenyon, 2007). Heick (2018) provides a schematic comparison of pedagogy, andragogy, and heutagogy. Table 3 compares some aspects of pedagogy, andragogy, and heutagogy.

Table 3. Pedagogy, andragogy, and heutagogy compared.

	Pedagogy	**Andragogy**	**Heutagogy**
Locus of control	(instructed)	Teacher/learner	Learner
Cognition level	Cognitive	Metacognitive	Epistemic
Learning mode	Rote learning	Single-loop learning	Double-loop learning
Outcome	Copying	Competence	Capability
Substance	Remembering	Understanding	Learning to learn
Questioning	What?	How?	Why?

Note. In this framework, andragogy reflects self-directed learning and heutagogy reflects self-determined learning.

Heutagogy

Heutagogy has been practiced by autodidacts for centuries ("Autodidacticism", n.d.). Ludwig von Mises remarked, "Many who are self-taught far excel the doctors, masters, and bachelors of the most renowned universities" (Mises,1957), as many innovations and discoveries were made by self-taught scientists. Even today, most PhD theses result from self-directed learning.

A key concept in heutagogy is that of double-loop learning and self-reflection as introduced by Argyris & Schön (1996). In double-loop learning, learners consider the problem and the resulting action and outcomes, in addition to reflecting upon the problem-solving process and how it influences each learner's own beliefs and actions. Double-loop learning occurs when learners, "question and test one's personal values and assumptions as being central to enhancing learning how to learn" (cited from Blaschke, 2012). This concept is illustrated schematically in Figure 2.

Figure 2. Single-loop and double-loop learning
(adopted from Blaschke, 2012).

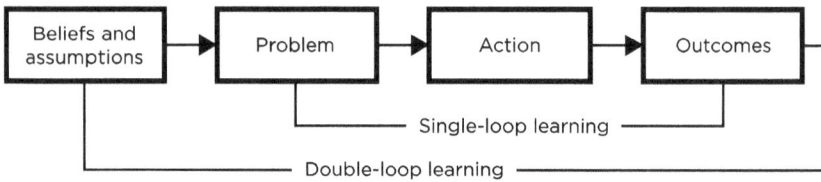

KT8302 - Rheology

The doctoral-level course, *KT8302 Rheology and Non-Newtonian Fluids*, had been taught for decades at Department of Structural Engineering, Norwegian University of Science and Technology. It followed a standard scheme: fixed curriculum, weekly lectures, minor assignments, and final assessment based on a written exam.

Rheology is the study of the deformation and flow of matter. We consider the subject demanding. Hence, the course attracted only a handful students, mainly foreigners. For some reason, in our experience, foreign students seem more dedicated to learn challenging subjects, while domestic (Norwegian) students appreciated opportunities to earn easier credits.

In the summer of 2014, the professor who taught the course fell from a ladder and broke his back while painting his house. Incapable of lecturing, he turned to a colleague for a helping hand. For practical purposes, the course was then changed into a heutagogical mould.

Realizing that just providing literature and telling students to learn rheology by themselves would never work on its own. Hence, a simple framework inspired by Seneca and Richard Feynman was adopted, covering three plenary sessions where at each session we gave the students teaching assignments applied to their own special field of research:

1. A Brief History of Rheology.
2. Main Rheology Models.
3. Rheology with Application to <own field of research>.

Figure 3. Progression from pedagogy to andragogy and heutagogy (adapted from Blaschke, 2012).

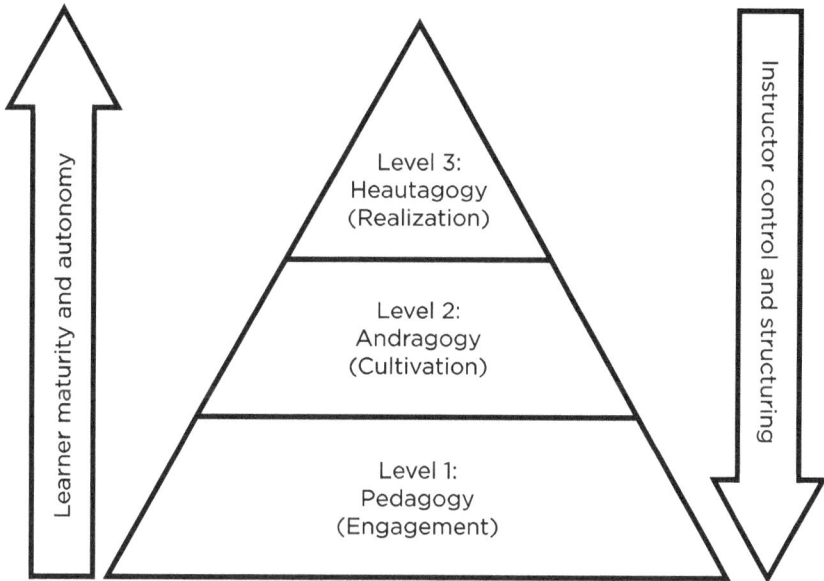

After each assignment students presented their own findings to each other using PowerPoint or similar presentation software. After the final session, we collected the printed assignments in a compendium "Rheology with Application to < own field of research>." The students have attained autonomy and matured their way of learning as illustrated in Figure 3.

Experiences

Over five years, the experience has been astonishing. Not only have the students lectures and compendia been excellent, students have explored new ways of learning extra-curricular topics and studied presentation techniques and writing, which in the long run may well turn out to be more useful to their future career than their knowledge of rheology. The course has gained a good reputation.

One student, who pursued a PhD at NTNU while working for a petroleum drilling company in Stavanger, could not present one of his assignments in class. Instead, he delivered a video presentation through the World Wide Web, which is now available on YouTube (Thoresen, 2016).

In fear of intervention from the university administrators, the course has been a quiet 'guerrilla endeavour.' The standard course procedure has not followed, as there has been no lectures and no formal exam.

In the first year (2014), a master's-level exchange student from Austria had been refused access to the course by the university administration. The rationale was that a master's student could not be allowed to follow a PhD-level course. Sadly, the neoliberal university has become a pure credit factory, and not a venue of learning.

We let him in, of course, promising to keep it a secret from the administration. On completion of the course, we issued a certificate he could bring back with him to Austria. He had performed extremely well, as his compendium on 'Rheology in polymer processing' demonstrates (Nindl, 2014). His joy of learning did not end with the course. The next spring, we received an email from him telling that the subject had been so inspiring that he had prepared a new, improved edition of his compendium.

A course website, opened during the fall term of 2018, may give an impression of a heutagogical approach to rheology (Syvertsen, 2018).

Conclusion

The Three Worlds of Karl Popper (1978) are:
- World 1 consists of physical bodies: of stones and of stars; of plants and of animals; but also of radiation, and of other forms of physical energy.
- World 2 is the mental or psychological world, the world of our feelings of pain and of pleasure, of our thoughts, of our decisions, of our perceptions and our observations; in other words, the world of mental or psychological states or processes, or of subjective experiences.
- World 3 is the world of the products of the human mind, such as languages; tales and stories and religious myths; scientific conjectures or theories, and mathematical constructions; songs and symphonies; paintings and

sculptures. But also, aeroplanes and airports and other feats of engineering. (Popper, 1978). World 3 is a physical representation of the mental World 2.

Five years of heutagogy in rheology have convinced us that students who are relieved of the straitjacket of lectures and exam will unleash a high potential of learning. The making of presentations introduces an aspect of the learning process that represents World 3 artifacts according to Karl Popper's theory, thereby reinforcing learning by feedback as illustrated in Figure 4.

Figure 4. Progression from pedagogy to andragogy and heutagogy (adapted from Blaschke, 2012**).**

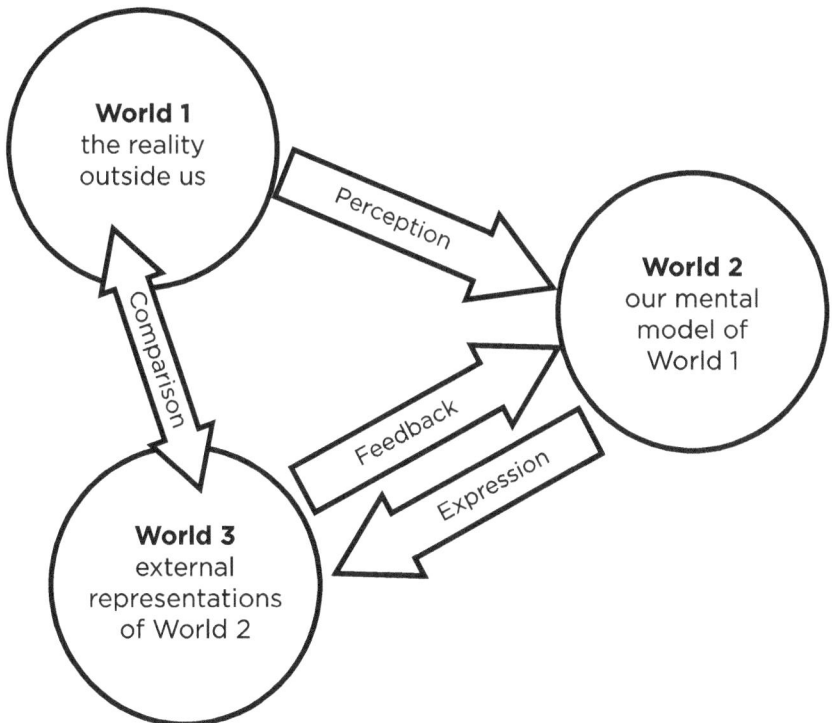

The significance of making World 3-artifacts for learning is also emphasized by Richard Feynman's statement, "What I cannot create, I do not understand" (Feynman, 1988). The idea is simple: presentation, discussion, and feedback make up a framework for double-loop learning.

This kind of sense-making is within the frame of the recent *knowledge-first* epistemology suggested by Williamson (2001,), "Knowledge and action are the central relations between mind and world. In action, world is adapted to mind. In knowledge, mind is adapted to world. When world is maladapted to mind, there is a residue of desire. When mind is maladapted to world, there is a residue of belief. Desire aspires to action; belief aspires to knowledge. The point of desire is action; the point of belief is knowledge" (p. 1). Figure 5 presents our concluding illustration of the concept.

Figure 5. The Mind in the world: the knowledge-action loop.

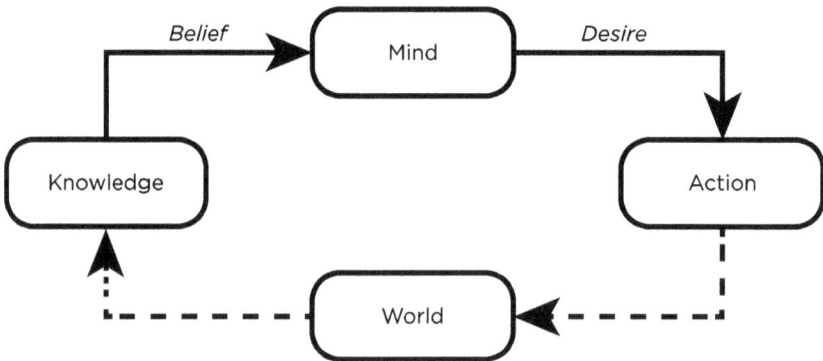

REFERENCES

Argyris, C. (1991). Teaching smart people how tolearn. *Harvard Business Review, 4*(2), 4-14. hbr.org/1991/05/teaching-smart-people-how-to-learn

Argyris, C., & Schön, D.A. (1996). *Organizational learning II: Theory, method, and practice.* Reading, MA: Addison.

Blaschke, L. (2012). Heutagogy and lifelong learning: A review of heutagogical practice and self-determined learning. *The International Review of Research in Open and Distributed Learning, 13*(1), 56-71. doi:10.19173/irrodl.v13i1.1076

Brandon, B. (2016). Two transformative learningstrategies: Heutagogy and personalization. www.learningsolutionsmag.com/articles/1912/two-transformative-learning-strategies-heutagogy-and-personalization

Center for Online Learning, Research and service, University of illinois, Springfield. (n.d.). Learning theories: Pedagogy, andragogy, and heutagogy compared. www.uis.edu/colrs/teaching/learning-theories/

Christensen, T. (2009): John Wheeler's mentorship: An enduring legacy: *Physics Today, 62*(4), 55; doi:10.1063/1.3120897

Farnam Street. (2012, April 26). The Feynman Technique: The best way to learn anything. fs.blog/2012/04/learn-anything-faster-with-the-feynman-technique/

Feynman, R. (1988, February). Photo of Richard Feynman's blackboard at time of his death. Pasadena, CA: Caltech Archives. archives-dc.library.caltech.edu/islandora/object/ct1%3A483

Hase, S., & Kenyon, C. (2007). Heutagogy: A child of complexity theory. *Complicity: An International Journal of Complexity and Education, 4*(1). doi:10.29173/cmplct8766

Hase, S., & Kenyon, C. (2000, December 14). From andragogy to heutagogy. Retrieved from: pandora.nla.gov.au/nph-wb/20010220130000/http://ultibase.rmit.edu.au/Articles/dec00/hase2.htm

Hase, S. (2016, May 5). Assessment driven learning: Not for the 21st century. heutagogycop.wordpress.com/2016/05/27/assessment-driven-learning-not-for-the-21st-century/

Hase S., & Kenyon, C. (2013, September 22). What is heutagogy?. www.slideshare.net/fredgarnett/selfdetermined-learning-the-craft-of-heutagogy

Heick, T. (2018, February 9). The difference between pedagogy, andragogy, and heutagogy. www.teachthought.com/pedagogy/a-primer-in-heutagogy-and-self-directed-learning/

von Mises, L. (1957). *Theory and history: An interpretation of social and economic evolution.* Auburn, AL: Ludwig von Mises Institute.

Nindl, M. (2014). Rheology in polymer processing. (Term Paper). Department of Structural Engineering, NTNU, Trondheim (2014).

Popper, K. (1978, April 7). Three worlds. tannerlectures.utah.edu/_documents/a-to-z/p/popper80.pdf

Syvertsen, T.G. (2018, September 19). KT8302 - Fall 2018. sites.google.com/site/kt8302fall2018/

Thoresen, K.E. (2016, October 06). History of rheology. Retrieved January 20, 2019, www.youtube.com/watch?v=Vt9LE2Ihow0

Westervelt, E. (2016, April 14). A Nobel laureate's education plea: Revolutionize teaching. *National Public Radio.* www.npr.org/sections/ed/2016/04/14/465729968/a-nobel-laureates-education-plea-revolutionize-teaching

Wikipedia. (2019, January 23). Autodidacticism. In *Wikipedia, The Free Encyclopedia.* en.wikipedia.org/wiki/Autodidacticism

Wikipedia. (2018, October 8). Docendo discimus. In *Wikipedia, The Free Encyclopedia.* en.wikipedia.org/wiki/Docendo_discimus

Williamson, T. (2001). *Knowledge and its limits.* Oxford: Oxford University Press

Erling N. Dahl, Einar N. Strømmen, and Tor G. Syvertsen are professors of structural engineering and engaged in learning without bureaucracy, each with over 40 years of experience in engineering, academic teaching, and research.

torgsyv@gmail.com

notes

Notes

notes

notes

Part II

Visions
&
ideas

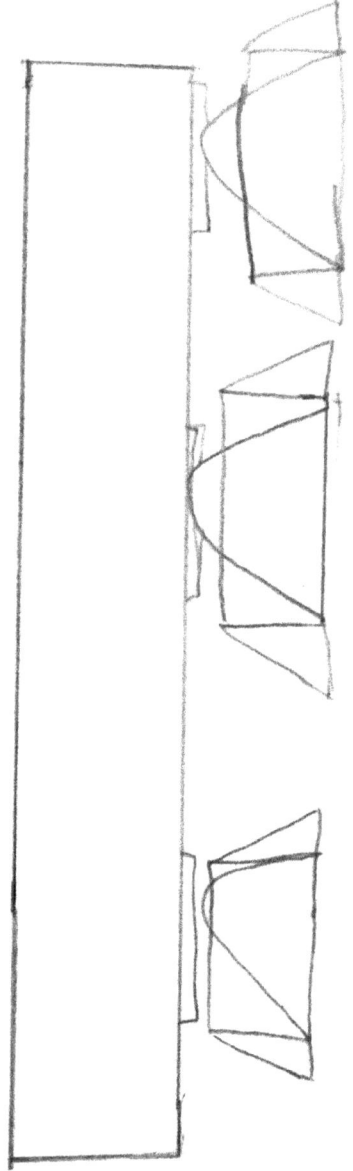

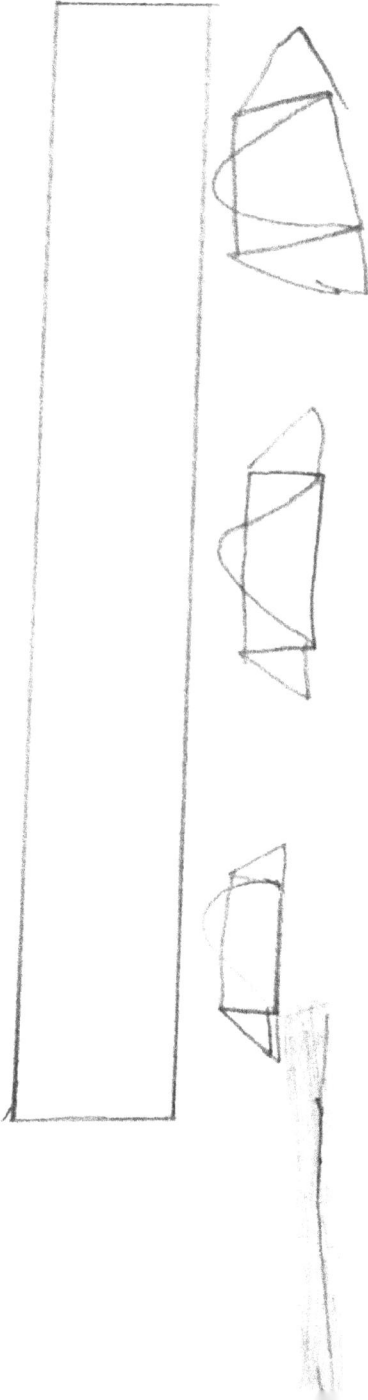

"KEY TO MY CLASSROOM OF THE FUTURE ARE THE DESKS, THE TELEVISION, AND THE **HEART**. THE DESKS ARE PUT TOGETHER AS A TABLE INSTEAD OF INDIVIDUAL STATIONS SO THE KIDS CAN SEE EACH OTHER AND TALK WITH EACH OTHER. THE CLASS SIZE IS SMALLER SO THE TEACHER HAS MORE TIME TO SPEND WITH EACH KID, AND THEY CAN DO MORE THINGS AS A GROUP. THE TV IS USED FOR TEACHING AND THE TEACHER MIGHT PUT A MOVIE ON WHEN EVERYONE'S DONE WITH THEIR HOMEWORK OR HAVE FREE TIME. THE **HEART** OF THE CLASSROOM IS THE BOND BETWEEN PEOPLE: STUDENTS AND THE TEACHER. THE **HEART** IS SOMETHING THE KIDS AND THE TEACHER KEEP FROM YEAR TO YEAR—PAST YEARS, NOW, AND FOREVER!"

Zoe Moravec (age 9)

Does the future need schools? What is education really for?

JOHN W. MORAVEC

KELLY E. KILLORN

What is the purpose of schools?

When we try to build an understanding of *what* we are educating for, *why* we do it, and *for whom* our educational systems serve, two paradigms of thought emerge. We frame the first on classical, Aristotelian ideals of academic *instruction* for the development of good citizens, critical thinking, and economic well-being (see esp. Locke, 1892;). The second is critical of the first, focused on *self-development*, arguing for liberation, democratization, and constructivist approaches for the individual learner (see esp. Freire, 2000; Gatto, 2003; von Glaserfeld, 1989; Gray, 2014). Given the friction between the two, one might expect a rich ecology of approaches to schooling, but such a rich ecology is absent from the world. Formal education has conformed itself. It seems we are trained to think and act in the first paradigm.

This is reflected in the modern approach to schooling with its structure of classrooms, age segregation, and testing. This model of universal education adopted worldwide is built from the Prussian system that emerged in the late 18th century and became codified in the early 18th century, which was intended to build loyal citizens who could serve as bureaucrats, industrial workers, and soldiers (Müller, 1989, pp. 18-23). But the world has transformed considerably since.

Summarizing the works gathered in their edited volume, Montgomery and Kehoe (2015) noted a sense of pessimism whether it is possible to re-imagine schools. Mainstream models, they argue, are built to resist different approaches, and it is difficult to imagine anything different (pp. 10-11). Viewing resistance to change as a pathways problem, if we are to imagine anything different, we believe it is important first to understand the purpose of schools. Are we still educating for the 18th century?

In March 2018, we emailed a message to selected contacts and followers on LinkedIn via email, and we sent similar messages via Twitter and Facebook, illustrated in Figure 6.

Figure 6. Survey invitation.

John Moravec at Education Futures   March 1, 2018 at 7:49 AM
Does the future need schools?
To: [invited participant]

Dear [firstname],

I need your help in finding answers to this short question:

Does the future need schools?
Why or why not?

As the future of work seems to become increasingly uncertain, schools charged with creating future-ready workers have changed very little over the past few centuries. A school from 2018 looks and functions little different than a school in 1918 would have operated. **As we look 10, 20, or 50 years into the future, will 'school' be relevant?**

10 years ago, I would have laughed at the question, but now I'm not sure. I'm reaching out to a select, diverse group of contacts from around the world to help bring some insight to the subject.

Please let me know what you think by taking a three-question survey at https://educationfutures.com/future-need-schools/.

This is an activity to generate an ecology of ideas for future research. All responses are confidential. You can read our research confidentiality and integrity statement at https://educationfu-tures.com/research/confidentiality/.

I estimate this should take just a minute or two of your time. Responses are due March 16, 2018.

Thank you in advance for sharing your insight!

John

The survey on the linked webpage was simple:

1. Does the future need schools? (yes/no, required response)
2. Optional: Why/why not? (optional)
3. In which industry do you primarily work? (optional)

The intent of the study was to provoke new thinking and responses on the research question of "what is the purpose of schools?" without asking the question directly and generate an ecology of ideas for analysis. Our operating theory is that we are trained to respond to the whys of schooling with instruction-based solutions for 18th century goals such as "to create good citizens" or "to prepare for entry into the workforce." But, if we were to ask "what is the purpose of school?" in an indirect (and provocative) way, we may get responses that are more thoughtful and independent of what we have been taught schooling is about.

As the purpose was to reveal ideas without focusing on measurement, survey protocol to allow generalizability of findings was not followed. The instrument was not piloted, and neither a pre-notice nor second notice were sent. As an arm's-reach study, recruiting out to followers on social media, this project was treated as an expert panel of people who are considered having put some thought into the topic before (at least by virtue of shared social media conversations) and could be considered in any study on the future of education. It was hoped that the less formal approach to the survey would provide a more candid and thoughtful responses as the invitation to participate was communicated as an act of personal outreach.

We received 164 responses in English and Spanish during the survey period of March 1-16, 2018. We scrubbed the resultant dataset to remove any identifying information (names, IP addresses, etc.) and employed an inductive strategy based on content analysis techniques described by Berg (2004, pp. 265-297) for grounded theory construction. We coded data to identify themes, with an emphasis on investigating the question, what is education really for?

Findings

Of the 164 total respondents, 116 (71%) said "yes," the future does need schools (Figure 7). 48 (29%) responded "no," the future does not need schools (Figure 8). Because of the nature of study, a statistical analysis of responses to this question by industry cannot be expected to provide reliable meaning, but it was interesting to note that among the respondents who said "yes," we recorded a relative increase in the number of higher education and retired people and a decrease in industry respondents, suggesting a split between these groups.

Figure 7. Distribution of industries for respondents who said, "yes, the future does need schools."

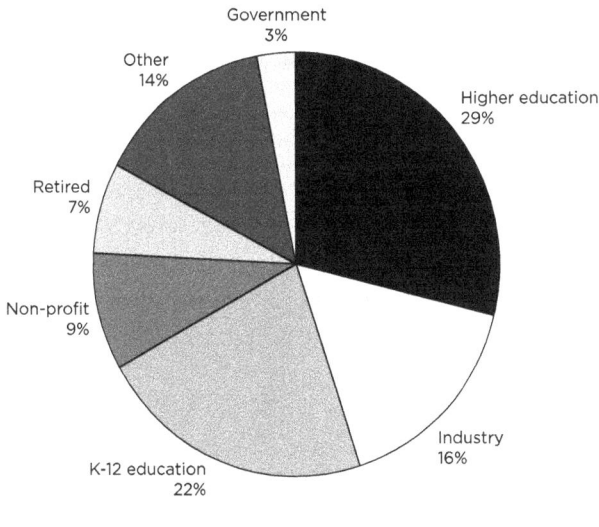

Figure 8. Distribution of industries for respondents who said, "no, the future does not need schools."

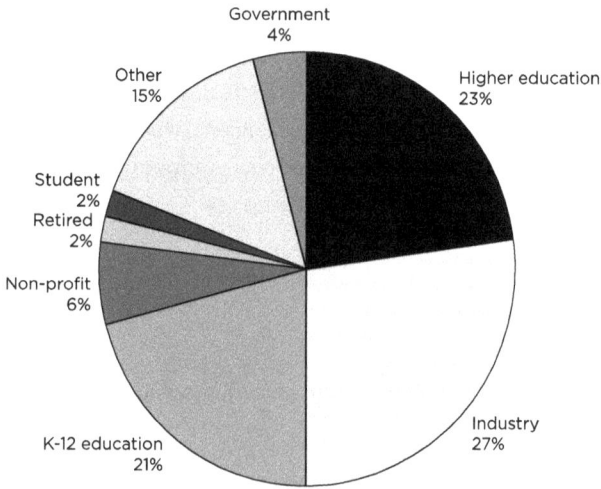

98% of respondents (161) answered the optional "why/why not?" question. We organized these into key themes that are summarized in Figure 9. Of the most significant themes, 17% related to the role of schools in providing socialization, 14% identified schools as a place for learning, 12% related to the idea that schools are obsolete, and 10% discussed that schools provide a structure for learning.

Minor themes that were organized into "other" include: schools enable young people; schools provide a base level of education for all children; we need innovative models; parents need help; schools serve as babysitters; children need to be told what to learn; schools educate citizens; schooling provides for the common good; schools improve the human experience; schools meet industry needs; and, we have no other option.

Figure 9. Key themes identified in survey responses.

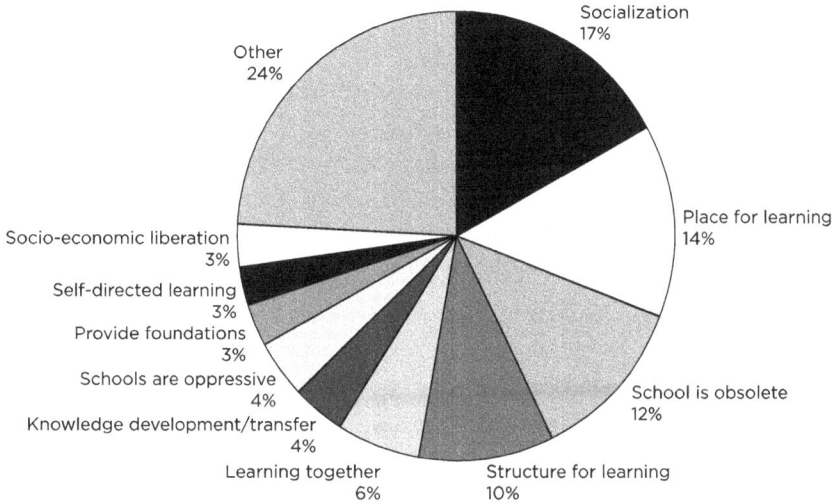

A detailed summary of our analysis is available as a mind map on the Education Futures website: https://educationfutures.com/schools-mindmap. We coded the analysis into areas of the purpose of school, current realities of schooling, learning environments, needs and characteristics of students and teachers, approaches to learning and teaching, and the future of school.

In identifying the purpose of school, respondents discussed its role in the development of knowledge and meeting real-life, current, and future needs. Education was described as a natural part of evolution, providing for social and political change, where participants can share, build, and grow ideas to lead toward a better society.

Schooling was argued as being more efficient than learning on one's own (or by families), but challenged by institutional resistance to change, age/grade separation, a focus on memorization, and its industrialized approach. Reported outcomes are that today's schools have become diploma factories where conservatism and conformity lead to low outcomes, but education nonetheless provides future opportunities for students to thrive in a rapidly transforming world.

As a learning environment, schools are overwhelmingly identified as a caring place to socialize, providing shelter, support, and stimulation for learning. As much as schools provide for a *place*, respondents often shared they believed there is no need for a building and that schooling can happen anytime and anywhere. Spaces are needed but must be suited for particular tasks as opposed to universal spaces such as school buildings. These spaces must provide equitable access for each learner where she or he can participate as a member of society.

Participants described students as mixed-age, multigenerational groups of individuals organized by interests. They have needs to be encouraged to become creative and unique individuals, and to develop themselves, personally, beyond what a school can traditionally provide. Students have social and emotional needs for human interaction, social involvement, positive relationships with others, and a place where they are cared about. There was disagreement, however, around learning needs. Some respondents reported that there are certain things that must be taught to children that require clarity and structure of schooling and that not every learner can learn by themselves. Others wrote that children often know concepts that adults do not know and that we can create value through face-to-face interactions between learners and mentors.

The majority of respondents who discussed the role of the teacher wrote about reorienting from a focus on teaching toward learning: working with students in multiple ways, engaging in more coaching, facilitating individual learning, and approaching schooling as a less-formal exercise. Participants often described teachers as mentors, guides, and consultants who are devoted toward helping students grow. Teachers need to expand their repertoire of tools and strategies, build flexibility to perform in different roles for each learner, and develop their intelligence as well—requiring new approaches to recruitment and training.

Most coded responses were centered on approaches to learning and teaching. Goals and outcomes should be real and involve students and communities in their determination. Formats for learning adopted by a school should be inquiry-based, focusing on solving problems to create new knowledge, utilizing a variety of approaches. It was reported these should focus on developing 'deep' learning that creates understanding, clarity, and meaning. As important as it is to focus on learning, several respondents also pointed out that unlearning is important and creating habits and practices for autodidactism.

Curricula should be focused on meeting the changing needs of society, provide liberation, generate basic training in skills and information, and, besides traditional skills such as literacy and math, provide for the development of skills such as digital literacy, digital ethics, storytelling, calculation, research, and connecting with nature. These require the development of new learning ecosystems that rely on less structure. Suggestions include deschooling (Illich, 1971), focusing on Internet-based learning, and eliminating classes, levels, subjects, schedules, and tests.

Numerous responses were related to the idea that learning is social (27 coded entries). Schools serve as communities of learning where students may solve problems together, reflect together, and learn from one another. Schools as learning communities must focus on developing students' individual-level knowledge and skills, leveraging the social experience. Approaches to learning include experiential learning (experimentation, workshops, simulations, and hands-on learning), free play and exploration (gathering, playing, and interacting around common interests), soft skills development (communication, creativity, collaboration, and critical thinking), and the development of agency: valuing all voices, thinking freely, and co-collaborating with teachers and students within democratic structures. This learning needs to be organized common values, interests, and creating positive experiences. Respondents further shared that schooling needs to meet social/emotional life skill needs as college/career skill development needs. Collections of experiences and competencies should replace diplomas, and while children need feedback from adults, formal grading is unnecessary.

Looking toward the future, respondents wrote that schools need to change. Society, technology, and how we work are changing, and the future will happen with or without our schools. Unless if they transform, several respondents wrote that schooling as an institution will become obsolete or "self-destruct" as a faulty design. Another asked, "does democracy need schools?"

Six respondents wrote that what a school is needs to be redefined, and others called for new terminology. New conceptualizations of school might become organically-evolving systems that can adapt to changing needs over time. At present, we design schools to be slow, and future structures need to adapt as fast in a world dominated by change, especially in the areas of innovation, knowledge, and technology. While several respondents wrote that functions and organization of schooling need to change, one respondent suggested we should reframe schooling from an institution into an activity. These transformations will require a new generation of trained people and funding to make it happen.

Response excerpts

The diversity and detail of the dataset pleased us and we found many of the responses to be profound. Here are a few that struck us the most, with some small fixes to grammar and citations added.

From a respondent who said *no, the future does not need schools*:

> *Does the future need schools? The future will find its form, anyway, whether there are schools or not. But I guess when you say 'future,' you think of an acceptable future for humankind. I think the future of humankind does not need schools; I think we will even be better off without. The question for societies is then: what will we do with all these wild, creative, rebellious, active, exploring young people in society? What will be their place, or even better: their role in the community of men if schools cease to exist?*

As Jean Pierre Lepri says, "schools are prisons, for the students as well as for the teachers. Democratic schools are nice prisons, but still prisons." We put in all this time and money and effort and good intentions in the educational system, but it is a crappy system and gets worse by the day. But the problem is: so many people are completely caught up in it and have their lives depend on it.

So on an individual scale school is a disastrous invention for many people (people being paid to do the job, convinced it is their responsibility to make others learn; and students, convinced they need these paid adults to learn in order to succeed in life). Everybody is unhappy in their role, and I think it does not help people to get the best out of their lives. So, I think for the future of the individuals involved, the best thing would be to quit, like deciding to break up a marriage that does not work.

On a society scale, I can see that schools are beneficial to society to a certain degree because of the structure. Society can use schools to get where it wants to get. It is an old rotten vehicle, but it still drives. Better an old car that's slow and does not steer very well than no car at all. Question: does democracy need schools?

Back to the future of humankind. Schools will pass; the educational system will implode, topple over; too much weight on a bad foundation. So I think it is time we start to think about what comes next. Not democratic education. Democratic education (I have been working in democratic education for the last 15 years) is a way to wake people up, but it is not the future. It is a step towards the grave of the educational system, but it will not carry us far into the future.

From a respondent who said *yes, the future needs schools*:

> *I believe school settings will experience disruptive changes, similar to the radical changes observed over the last two decades in creative companies' workspaces.*
>
> *As stated by Clark Aldrich in his book Unschooling rules (2011), today "what a person learns in a classroom is how to be a person in a classroom" (p. 23), and "the only sustainable answer to the global education challenge is a diversity of approaches" (p. 143).*
>
> *[...] Our current education system has its roots in the industrial age society. Today, students are much more social and enjoy learning in a less structured way, anytime, anywhere. Learning is no longer limited to the confines of a traditional classroom.*
>
> *The new learning space environment shall offer a variety of settings, as catalysts for changing classrooms into authentic research & experimentation workshops, moving away from the post-industrial revolution settings, conceived for mass production.*
>
> *This change in structure will emphasize the concept that the school student is at the core of the learning experience, rather than the teacher. Educators will then focus on what matters most: creating opportunities and environments in which students learn and thrive, establishing the foundation of a learner-centric education.*

And, another respondent who said *yes, the future needs schools*:

> *At the elementary level, schools act as in loco parentis. Many children need an adult in their lives when responsible parenting is absent. Schools provide a shelter and caring environment when this is missing. Schools act as in loco parentis and provide opportunities to develop social, group, and communication skills. Ideally, they are a respite from less than ideal home and neighborhood environments. At the secondary level, schools need to provide relevant vocational skills for those who may not think a college track is for them. Secondary schools need to revamp their curricula with proper funding to realize variation in curricula. At the college level, and I will use a personal example, my family never attended college and most didn't complete a 4-year high school curriculum. Therefore, college was never encouraged and upon high school graduation I did not have a clue as to my future. Attending college following military service opened up a world to me I never knew. The idea of sharing ideas with other students is something I'll always cherish. Yes, schools are necessary, but schools need to adapt to change.*

Finally, from a respondent who said *no, the future does not need schools*:

> *John, You're asking the wrong question. The question should be, "in the future, what role will the school play in preserving and building our society?" There will always be a 'need' for schools- 10 years, 20 years, 50 years and beyond. Humankind is inherently social. It's built into our DNA. From its very foundation, schools have served the role of providing a social setting through which children can learn how to assimilate into a broader society. Initially, it centered around teaching the '3r's' at a level sufficient to allow them to interact capably in a marketplace and be self-sufficient. School buildings*

weren't necessary. Churches would do; incorporating a system of instilling values into one's character. Eventually, as societal needs changed, curriculum and instruction followed-historically it's never led. Industrial age brought industrial age buildings; replicas of the manufacturing world. Soon, buildings came to 'represent' schools and all that went into them. Today, the question of the need for schools only arises because of the focus and interdependence of curriculum, instruction and facilities. Once this relationship is broken, the more appropriate question of "what role the school will play in the future?" can be addressed. Recognizing the social nature of our inner being and the 'breakdown' of the 19th and 20th century family, a place where children can gather will always be a necessity. What happens in that 'place' will differ than what we call a school today. This new place will need to provide socialization opportunities; aided by facilitators and experts in this area. This new place will provide opportunities for learning, learning in ways beyond simple 'sit and git' as well as beyond 'stare, glare, and prepare.' This place called school will include planned opportunities for children (and adults in need of retooling) to collaborate on areas of particular interest. It will be a place where community resources will be found, available and used. It will be a place to share, build and grow ideas that will lead to a better society and world to live in. So, does the future need schools? Yes, just a lot different!

Conclusions

Yes, we can generate an ecology of ideas around the purpose of schools and education when we frame the question differently. Is the future focused on *instruction* or is the future focused on *self-development*? The data we received support the theory that we can break away from our trained responses of why we engage in schooling and the purpose of education. Ideas centered on creating good citizens or preparation for entry into the workforce were not coded into any main response category. 43% (70 responses) called for a need to change or evolve education. 13% (22 responses) provided specific ideas, examples, or pathways for changing or evolving schooling. And, only 3% (5 responses) expressed sarcasm (e.g., "how else, other than schools, can we as a society so effectively crush creativity and train the next generation of bureaucratic laborers?"), reflecting a high level of thoughtfulness.

An interesting idea that emerged in the data is that we are perhaps limited in our shared vocabulary in how we work with topics of teaching, learning, and schooling. The implication is that legacy concepts surrounding education have become so ingrained into our language and how we think we struggle to understand ourselves and communicate with others as we look toward building new approaches to education for the future.

While we can expect retired respondents would hold a more-traditional perspective and be more likely to respond yes, the future needs schools, we found it interesting to note growth of respondents from higher education also saying *yes, the future needs schools*. As tertiary-level institutions are usually responsible for teaching teachers, school leaders, and policymakers, additional, detailed research into the differences between K-12 and higher education professionals could provide insight into potential discrepancies into how each group perceives the purpose of schools.

REFERENCES

Aldrich, C. (2011). *Unschooling rules: 55 ways to unlearn what we know about schools and rediscover education*. Austin, TX: Greenleaf.

Berg, B.L. (2004). *Qualitative research methods for the social sciences* (5th ed.). Boston: Pearson.

Freire, P. (2000). *Pedagogy of the oppressed* (30th anniv. ed.). New York: Continuum.

Gatto, J.T. (2003). *The underground history of American education*. New York: Oxford Village Press.

Von Glaserfeld, E. (1989). Cognition, construction of knowledge and teaching. *Synthese, 80*(1), 121-140. files.eric.ed.gov/fulltext/ED294754.pdf

Gray, P. (2014). *Free to learn*. New York: Basic Books.

Illich, I. (1971). *Deschooling society*. New York: Harper & Row.

Lock, J. (1892). *Some thoughts concerning education*. Cambridge, UK: Cambridge University Press. books.google.com/books?id=YCsWAAAAIAAJ

Montgomery, A., & Kehoe, I. (Eds.). (2015). *Reimagining the purpose of schools and educational organisations: Developing critical thinking, agency, beliefs in schools and educational organisations*. Cham: Springer.

Müller, D.K. (1989). The process of systemisation: The case of German secondary education. In. Müller, D.K., Ringer, F., & Simon, B. *The rise of the modern educational system: Structural change and social reproduction* (pp. 15-52). Cambridge/Paris: Cambridge University Press/Editions de la Maison des Sciences de l'Homme.

John W. Moravec is researcher on the future of work and education, a global speaker, and the founder of Education Futures LLC. His work focuses on exploring new approaches to leadership and human capital development required to build positive futures in a society dominated by accelerating technological and social change.
john@educationfutures.com

Kelly E. Killorn is a literacy specialist with over 20 years of experience in public education at the primary and secondary levels. She is a teacher leader in Bloomington Public Schools (Minnesota) and works to enhance the performance of in-service teachers at Hamline University.
kellykillorn@gmail.com

NOTES

Notes

Notes

Notes

Affordances of pedagogy

PEKKA IHANAINEN

Introduction

Affordances for learning as originally developed by James J. Gibson (see esp. Gibson, 1979; Ihanainen,1992; Hinton, 2014) are functionalities composed by human subjects in their personal and social contexts and environments in which they make their living. Pedagogical affordances are those present in pedagogical events and situations, and they determine the qualities of learning possible in practices learners localize themselves. In this chapter, the most relevant affordances for authentic pedagogy are proposed to be *observability* (especially within traditional schools), *partakeability* (within democratic schools for example) and *solvability* (e.g., in project-, problem-, and phenomenon-based learning). These pedagogical affordances (and their adverse counterparts: *non-observability*, *non-partakeability*, *non-solvability*) are present in all pedagogical practices, and a key issue is to create an awareness of them and their complex power to make learning successful, either for constructive knowledge development or for resistant and evading activities.

Affordances

Affordances are real objects, places, and events that *afford*—that is, they make it possible to do something. They are functionalities in which one thinks, feels, and acts. A physical object, like a chair, makes sitting possible or someone may use it as a platform to reach something. But a chair does not afford the possibility of flying. Affordances allow only certain, even unexpected activities, but not every activity. Places such as a physical or virtual classroom or a street or forest provide more complex affordances, but, in principle, they only make some orientations and activities to happen in them possible. And a situation is the same with events like a TED Talks performance, concert, or moose hunting in real or online environments.

Affordances become more complex, especially when people enter them. Objects, places, and events become social affordances. The potential functionalities in them afford shared cognitive, affective, and intentional activities. A good example of this is expressed in social media behavior research by Davis & Chouinard (2017), in which a complex affordance can be found for example in requesting (signing up Facebook request a profile image), demanding (Facebook demands to select a gender before signing up), and encouraging (like and share options in Facebook encourage network interaction) artifacts. Requesting demanding, encouraging etc. form a complicated social affordance.

Figure 10. Observability, partakeability, and solvability are fundamental pedagogical affordances, which make successful teaching, learning, and project work possible.

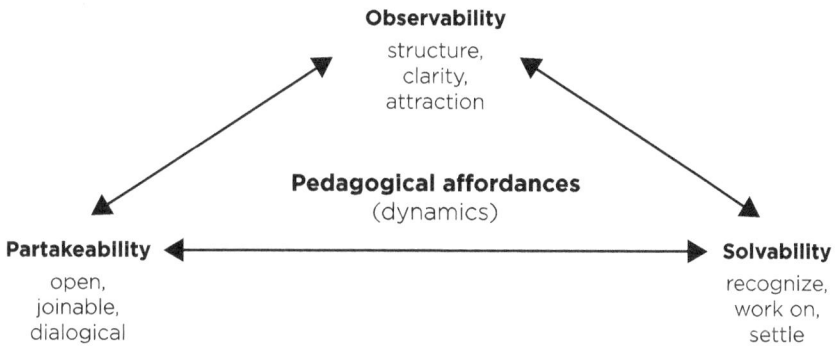

Observability
structure,
clarity,
attraction

Pedagogical affordances
(dynamics)

Partakeability
open,
joinable,
dialogical

Solvability
recognize,
work on,
settle

Table 4. Affordance functionalities.

Pedagogical affordance	Basic functionality
Observability	What can I get out of teaching? (teacher-driven education)
Partakeability	How can I make learning happen in collaboration with others? (learner-driven education)
Solvability	How can I learn, as an individual or group, by examining questions and problems? (problem-driven education)

Learning and teaching contexts are full of both single affordances and complex, dynamic affordance structures. The pedagogical point is that social affordances—in both good or bad manifestations—define (or at least compose) learning and teaching behavior. It is the reason to request educators to know and understand the meaning and role of pedagogical affordances in their daily work.

Pedagogical contexts

We may define pedagogical contexts, for example, on the basis of formality. Moravec (2013) notes that *invisible learning* covers non-formal, informal, and serendipitous learning. Formal learning and education is the sphere we all are familiar with. It is the bedrock of traditional schools with teacher-driven lessons, formal curriculum, and test based assessment. Non-formal learning is more organized, and it takes place outside the formal education system. For instance, one may consider democratic schools centered within this pedagogical context. Informal and serendipitous learning belong more or less to the field of *open learning and pedagogy*, which are based on the autonomy of learners, bolstered by peer and collegial support.

It is possible to elaborate on three different kinds of pedagogical contexts described above. They are traditional schools, organized, learner-centered learning venues such as democratic schools, and open learning settings in which authentic problems, phenomena, interests, and self-organized projects comprise a context for learning and collegial (peer-to-peer) pedagogy. These pedagogical contexts may overlap many times, especially within endeavors to develop new educational practices. However, when examined from a sufficiently general level, they emerge as three different pedagogical contexts, which may be studied through developed pedagogical affordances.

Pedagogical affordances

A teacher-driven, traditional school activity is based mainly on affordances of observability. Democratic schools and corresponding institutions run their activities within the scope of partakeability, which forms a grounded affordance structure for them. Teaching and learning that emphasizes authenticity in open situations roots itself within an affordance of solvability.

In traditional schools, we base education on teaching by teachers. The teacher teaches and demonstrates. The affordance of observability in this case is focused in how teaching become visible, reachable and understandable and how the teacher is felt present with the topic and by the learning audience.

In democratic schools, learners decide objectives, content, methods, and pace of activity in learning events. Teachers are present to support the learning process. Here, the affordance of partakeability provides opportunities and abilities to ideate, plan, and create and make new knowledge together.

In open learning situations, certain phenomena, topics, or cases become important to examine. They can happen on their own or a facilitator can try to trigger 'a problem' for people (learners) present in the situation. Here, the affordance of solvability provides factors and practicalities through which we can recognize and identify any phenomenon, topic, or case and then move forward as a target for examination and execution. For example, a group of primary school aged learners may realize that they have to deepen their understanding about percentage calculation. They have been in a situation in which they (probably facilitated by a teacher, coach, etc.) have to know better how much something is from a bigger amount of a certain substance. They identify the case, figure out what has to do to work out the issue, and then to solve the case. This kind of learning event includes solvability affordance dynamics.

Observability

Observability characterizes qualities of teacher-centered education, which manifests itself especially in traditional, mainstream schools. The success of pedagogical practice in school rests on possibilities and abilities to follow-up the teaching given and led by teachers. As an affordance, this opportunity for action (i.e., to follow a teacher's performance) by complementary humans (i.e., students complementing the teaching by being able to observe it) provides observability. Observability also encompasses three sub-affordances. They are *structuredness*, *clarity*, and *attractiveness*.

Structuredness refers to a teacher's activities, which include the integrated dynamics of content, phases of content presentation (beginning, episodes, ending), and cognitive, affective, and intentional elements of content. *Clarity* defines how connections between the presentation ensemble and sections are put forth, and how we can perceive and understand phases of the presentation. The mental structure (cognitive elements, etc.) of a teaching-learning approach to content informs how the pedagogical event touches overall and unique human qualities of learners.

This is a part of *attractiveness* contained in observability. Besides cognitive, affective, and intentional elements of teaching performances, attractiveness bears a personal presence of the content presenter. That is, how she or he carries her or his real being in the teaching and learning event.

Structuredness, clarity, and attractiveness have their opposite counterparts. Structuredness, when it does not exist in practice, or when it is vague, becomes unstructured and produces resistance. If the audience cannot perceive and understand the assumed structure of a presentation easily enough (e.g., a lecture or lesson), it causes frustration and active or passive resistance. We may label it as a *resistibility* affordance.

Clarity is a sub-affordance of observability. If clarity does not come true, and this obscurity disturbs following the teaching, it means that the presentation does not touch or move. It causes a loss of enthusiasm in the sense of lack of interest to trying to understand. This counterpart to the affordance of clarity is *apathy*.

If the sub-affordance of attractiveness is absent from the practice of teaching (i.e., if learners do not feel a presenter is 'present'), this brings forth passive and evasive behavior. The teacher does not attract learners, but she/he is perceived as aversive. As an affordance, this means *evasiveness*.

The pedagogical affordance of observability exists as a complex of affordances. Its dynamics consist of tensions between structuredness-resistibility, clarity-apathy and attractiveness-evasiveness. This social affordance of observability gives learners an opportunity to follow or not to follow the teaching or to vacillate back and forth in between different dynamic states.

Figure 11. Observability dynamics.

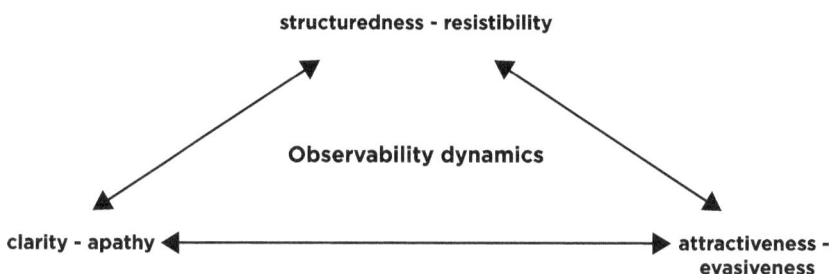

A clear example of the observability affordance having a success effect is Kawasaki's '10/20/30 rule' for a good presentation (see e.g. Schofield, n.d.): ten slides, twenty minutes in total duration, and use of a thirty-point font. This approach nicely includes structure and clarity in themselves, and if the presenter speaks on the theme she or he is enthusiastic about, the presenter is more likely to attract the audience. It is also easy to imagine a presenter submerged into a mass of unthinkable slides. Here, there is no other option, but to resist, feel droopy, and evade the learning 'experience.'

Partakeability

Partakeability evokes participatory activity. It is more than pure inclusiveness as open and inviting access to learning-teaching events. Partakeability encourages *and even demands* active participation from learners to make and do, to collaborate, and to interact.

Partakeability also comprises of three sub-affordances, which are *openness, joinability*, and *dialogicality*. *Openness* refers to unique events of participation that are neither restricted nor coordinated in any way. Attendance depends only on learners' and teachers' initiatives and their situational motivation to take part together.

Joinability grows from openness. When learners feel welcome to take part, they are willing to affiliate with an ongoing activity or initiative. They want to join it. Openness and joinability form a continuum, which culminates in conversations and dialogue. *Dialogicality* elevates participants' learning through responsive meeting and interaction.

Figure 12. Partakeability dynamics.

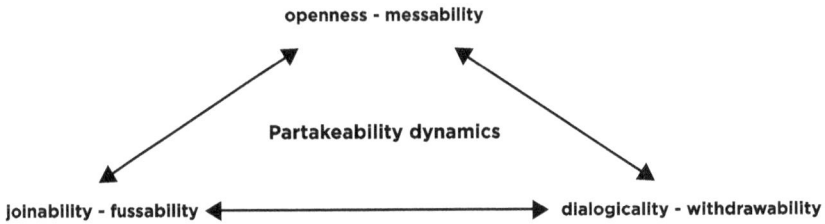

Partakeability has its counterparts as well. The learning-teaching event can afford participants not only to take part responsively but also to disturb, harass, and mess around; or, to prevent joining and instead fuss and bustle learning activities; or, to hamper discussion and to push learners to withdraw from shared participation to peoples' own doings and jobs or just to stay mentally within the confines of their own worlds.

Openness has its counterpart in an affordance of *messing around*, joinability in *fussability*, and dialogicality in *withdrawability*. The composition of the affordance of partakeability manifests in the dynamics of openness-messability, joinability-fussability, and dialogicality-withdrawability. It requires pedagogical knowledge and expertise to recognise the dynamics of this affordance and to work toward constructive partakeability.

When learners can appreciate themselves and they feel acknowledged and respected as who they are, they normally may openly join with each other and start discussions. In some Finnish schools, students and teachers intend to start their study periods by meeting together in the entrance and activity hall or another corresponding space, and then check-in with each other as to what their study situations are in terms of learning and study needs. Based on this 'analysis,' future learning activities are discussed and determined in small groups and individually. And, when they are accepted jointly, learning endeavours are put into practice. This example depicts how the affordance of partakeability can drive learner-driven pedagogy. If the created learning space is poorly facilitated, or it grows spontaneously, it is easy to imagine that the activity venue can become messy, bustling, and it would invite one to withdraw.

Solvability

Solvability, as an affordance, speaks about situations in which an activity is to take place, a problem is to be worked on, or in which there is a phenomenon to grasp that is potentially and temptingly present. Solvability also includes elements of observability and partakeability; it cannot exist without them. Yet, solvability is more than a sum of the other two affordances.

Solvability is an affordance that is intentional and goal-oriented. When individuals and groups, through observing factors, situations, problems, etc., share their observations with others and take part in working together, they perceive and realize the potential of reaching the goal or target at hand. They are in touch with the solvability of the case. They are within the realm of possibility via shared processes (shared with people and/or some other available resources) to find an outcome or a solution that is desired.

The affordance of solvability includes sub-affordances of *recognizability* of problems presented by the case (a modification of observability), *work-onability* of the case (a modification of partakeability), and, as a way to trace, analyze and conclude the case, *traceability*. The sub-affordances of recognizability, work-onability, and traceability have their counterparts similarly, as does observability and partakeability. The sub-affordance of recognizability, to have an image of the case, if it is not clear enough, leads to an unnamed case, or it challenges a learner to raise alternative interpretations and conceptions to see and name the case (*alternativity*). The work-onability, if it is difficult to carry it intentionally on, tempts to pace for doing things, which are not valid with the case (*invalidity*). The path to trace the case, if it does not open up fairly enough, leads to alienation and also to activity not relevant with the immediate case (*alienating*). As a result, the potential solution runs away to peripheral and apparent procedures and outcomes not significant for resolving the case.

Solvability affords constructive activities to meet a challenge—that is, to name and work on it, and to make conclusions. But it also can lead to actions to review and orient for resolving the case anew, providing more diverse options to original case situation. And, when the solvability entirely bends to its counterpart, it affords unsettledness.

Figure 13. Solvability dynamics.

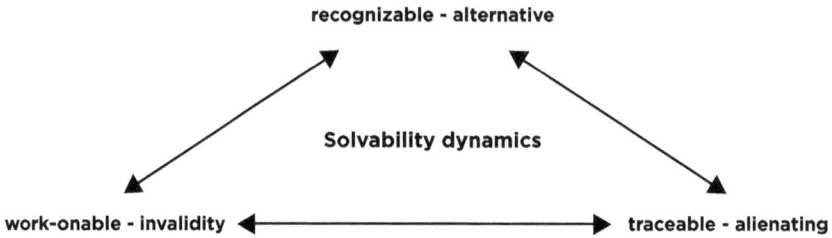

The affordance dynamics in which solvability implements itself can move more or less simultaneously in transitions from recognizable to alternative, from work-onable to invalid and from traceable to alienating keeping still itself as one solvability affordance. Educators should be aware of these affordance dynamics and have competences to facilitate them in learning situations and to make actions within it.

An event which aims toward a goal-oriented outcome or toward the solution of a problem can accidentally emerge from an ongoing teacher-centered or learner-centered activity, or people (learners) present in the situation can purpose and intentionally define it. Since the beginning of 2019, learners and teachers may have been in a situation in which they have had to decide whether to participate in a school-wide protest for climate (a student strike). They have had to discuss, collect relevant information and knowledge, and decide for or against their involvement. This examined as an example of an affordance of solvability includes factors and functionalities to recognize the school strike phenomena in question or to figure out alternatives for it. It also consists of working on to argue the rationality for the proposed school strike or to sink toward invalidating the idea by working through arguments. Finally, it encloses the conclusion process to attend to the school strike or, on the contrary, to feel it incomprehensible and alienating because it is not understood.

Teacher-driven pedagogy

The affordance of observability especially defines a teacher-driven pedagogy. Teachers are at the top of the relationship, and the success or failure of this pedagogical approach depends on how teachers make the observability true in practice.

The teacher-driven pedagogy starts when a teacher enters the learning-teaching venue. His or her attractiveness or evasiveness creates the learning atmosphere. The teacher's warm-up activities continue the construction of a unique learning space. They make it compelling or unattractive.

Introductions to teaching content is the next phase in a teacher-driven pedagogy. Now, clarity and the structure of the teacher's presentations are the key factors to keep the performance motivating and interesting. If the teacher fails, the observability bends toward apathy and resistance. When the teacher keeps the observability constructive, learning-teaching activities may proceed to interactive and participatory activities. This means moving to more learner-driven approaches to working.

Learner-driven pedagogy

In learner-driven pedagogy, the teacher's role is to serve as a facilitator who personally meets learners, says, "hello," listens, and thus creates an open, free, and respectful learning space in which discussions about learning and other activities may take place. This, of course, may happen without facilitation by the teacher if learners are comfortable in joining the work in learning and can study on their own.

When learners interact and collaborate, the teacher's task is to support dialogical activities of the learners for whom they are responsible. If the learning group fails with the help of a teacher in openness, joining, and dialogue, the learning space regresses to variations of learners' jamming and fussing behavior, and even toward withdrawal from adequate learning activities.

In successful learner-driven learning, teachers may offer 'their own' learning content to the process which they believe to be relevant and important for the learning situation, to be included in 'the partakeability.'

Project-driven pedagogy

Project-driven pedagogy, when it works well, has in its background positive achievements in maintaining activities for observability and partakeability. In other words, teacher-driven and learner-driven approaches have been rewarding in earlier learning-teaching events and experiences of learners and teachers. They already are capable of using the affordances of observability and partakeability. Observability and partakeability keep in themselves a motivating factor for project-driven pedagogy.

This motivational learning culture gives space for defining cooperatively at the beginning of a project and then execution tasks successfully together. The tasks include possible divisions of labour and agreements of individual and collaborative contributions to finish the project in alignment with the expected project outcomes. Project-driven pedagogy also affords the possibility to identify and update the project anew, if it seems reasonable, and then again continue collaborative and individual activities needed for completing the project.

A well-working, project-driven pedagogy identifies solvability for its affordance dynamics. Recognizability, work-onability, and traceability are necessary in project-driven pedagogy. Updates and redefinitions may be consequences of alternativity, invalidity, and alienation, but they also can cause the project to fail. The failure thus may engender a new start for the project, but also lead to disaster and disappointment to the pedagogical effort.

The teacher's role in project-driven pedagogy is to keep the affordance of solvability existent by arranging the project space, and by providing supportive and confronting facilitation acts during the project work constructively. The teacher should behave simultaneously as a peer and an occasional team leader to return the conduct of the project back to learners as soon as possible.

Epilogue

The essence of an affordance is that although it is an objective fact in a social environment, it simultaneously is subjective. For instance, observability, partakeability, and solvability affordances exist in pedagogical contexts - either "for good or bad," as Gibson put it - although I do not perceive and realize them being there. And still affordances always include subjects within them as social affordances. Affordance despite me (or us) are true only as functional constructs or possibilities for action for perceivers, experiencers, and doers.

If we think of observability, partakeability, and solvability affordances developed in this chapter, they always exist somehow in a pedagogical context, even if some people cannot connect with them. To reach these affordances, learners and teachers need to have the ability to capture them. Teachers, together with other learning providers and supporters, should be able to detect affordances within learning environments and to enhance learning spaces that carry constructive functionalities of observability, partakeability, and solvability. That is to say, we can learn affordances through the detection of the learning flow and pedagogical context.

This requires a new mindset for educators. The understanding of affordances means developing abilities to perceive and act with functionalities in structure, clarity and attraction, openness, joining and dialogue dynamics, and problems in terms of recognizing, working on and resolving the case at hand. The essential element within affordances is that—learned or not to detect and be powered with—they are still 'over there' and out of reach if they are not realized. Affordances (including pedagogical ones) are objective-subjective functional realities, and the task of learners and teachers is to become familiar with them and to enhance education practices through awareness and knowhow. Learners and educators must trust in the authenticity of learning and develop their perceptual acuity to align and attune within existent learning environments and events (Gallagher, Ihanainen, 2015). This also challenges pedagogical orientations to examine teacher-driven, learner-driven and project-driven practices anew and their complex dynamics as pedagogical affordances.

REFERENCES

Davis, J., & Chouinard, J. (2017). Theorizing affordances: From request to refuse. www.academia.edu/33562886/Theorizing_Affordances_From_Request_to_Refuse.pdf

Gallagher, M., & Ihanainen, P. (2015). Aesthetic literacy: Observable phenomena and pedagogical applications for mobile lifelong learning (mlll). *European Journal of Open, Distance and e-Learning*, *18*(1). www.degruyter.com/downloadpdf/j/eurodl.2015.18.issue-1/eurodl-2015-0002/eurodl-2015-0002.pdf

Gibson, J.J. (1979). *Ecological approach to visual perception.* Boston: Hougton Mifflin.

Hinton, A. (2014). *Understanding context.* Sebastopol, CA: O'Reilly. www.oreilly.com/library/view/understanding-context/9781449326531/

Ihanainen, P. (1992). School and instruction - are they revolutionary improvable. www.slideshare.net/pekkai/schoolandinstruction-aretheyrevolutionarilyimprovable-091201141313-phpapp01

Moravec, J.W. (Ed.). (2013). *Knowmad Society.* Minneapolis: Education Futures.

Schofield, J. (n.d.). If You Learn This 10-20-30 Rule, Every Presentation You Give Will Be Excellent. www.lifehack.org/518746/if-you-learn-this-10-20-30-rule-every-presentation-you-give-will-be-excellent

Pekka Ihanainen is an emeritus teacher educator from Haaga-Helia University in Helsinki, Finland. He also works as an educational entrepreneur, focusing on guidance and counseling phenomena and activities in the fields of education and workplace enhancement. He is especially interested in developing learner-driven facilitation methods, personalization, learning design, and aesthetic literacy discourse on broadening and deepening multi-literacy and phenomenon-based learning approaches in formal and informal education. He also serves as a volunteer for Teachers Without Borders, Finland.
ihanainenpekka@gmail.com

Notes

Notes

notes

Notes

Multiliteracies dynamic affinity spaces:

Analysing the potential of a new framework to educate for Knowmad Society

STEFANIA SAVVA

This chapter is a discursive response to the discussions and ideas proposed by Cristóbal Cobo in *Knowmad Society* (2013) in an attempt to address the "skills and competencies for knowmadic workers." Cobo (2013, p. 59), seeks to "explore and outline, the conditions required to foster critical skills, such as problem-solving, reflection, creativity, critical thinking, learning to learn, risk-taking, collaboration, and entrepreneurship." Here, I try to map the landscape of a pedagogical approach that would frame the kind of education expected to nurture the critical skills mentioned above and break through the *educational iceberg.* Cobo (2013, p.59) suggests five trends to explore the conditions necessary to ensure "multi-skilled profiles" and "multi-contextual learning practices":

- The mismatch between formal education and the challenges of the innovation society (informal and flexible learning approaches);
- The shift from what we learn to how we learn (lifelong, self-learning, and learning to learn);
- The fluctuating relationship between digital technologies and content (ICT and critical thinking skills and new literacies);
- The changing conceptions of space-time and a lifelong learning environment (which is rarely time or context dependent); and,
- The development of soft skills (global, tacit, and social).

In this narrative, I address the aforementioned five trends in respect to a specific educational approach, namely the *multiliteracies dynamic affinity spaces* (MDAS) framework, proposed as the theoretical backdrop on which to educate the Knowmad Society. The MDAS framework is a theory-based, empirically-driven foundation, informing my instructional planning and design over the course of my doctoral and postdoctoral research. The framework draws on the role of technology in providing differentiated instruction and ways to capitalize on the potential multiliteracies surrounding us, to develop flexible, multi-skilled learners.

The MDAS in particular, relies on a creative overlap between the theory of the New London Group (1996) for a pedagogy of multiliteracies and the theory of affinity spaces proposed by Gee (2004). In 2016, I contributed a chapter for a book edited by Anthony Montgomery and Ian Kehoe, entitled *Reimagining the purpose of schools and educational organisations* (2016). The book features a diverse set of perspectives, all focused on questioning the role schools play in society and the role they might play. I specifically addressed the need to re-conceptualize schooling through a multiliteracies affinity lens for it to be relevant and responsive to "evolving ways of communication, interpretation and creation of meaning, which change the learning demands and needs of individuals" (Savva, 2016a, p. 46).

To examine the feasibility of the framework adopted for re-imagining schooling, I used a vignette. The core of this work draws on my doctoral and postdoctoral research into technology-enhanced learning for culturally and linguistically diverse students, through a synergy of formal and informal learning principles. The text that follows is not a summary of that research, but an expanded discussion of the ideas and interpretations that followed this implementation and evaluation of the theory-driven framework. In this respect, I hope that my viewpoints, being both a primary teacher and a researcher, will offer some insights into the potential of a particular framework to improve education for Knowmad Society.

Weaving the big picture

Before I begin to address how the MDAS framework meets the different conditions that are necessary for educating to ensure "multi-skilled profiles" and "multi-contextual learning practices," I provide three important definitions on literacy, multiliteracies, and affinity spaces. Throughout this discussion, I use the term literacy to refer to "the flexible and sustainable mastery of a repertoire of practices with the texts of traditional and new communication technologies via spoken, print, and multimedia" (Luke & Freebody, 2000, p. 9). The nature of literacy practice and needs has shifted; no longer is the traditional view of literacy as reading and writing skills acceptable (Fleming, 2005, p. 114). Both literacy pedagogy and research now embrace the idea of literacy as more of a plurality, discussing various 'literacies' (Liddicoat, 2007, p. 15).

The most pertinent and influential theory which has shaped the discussion in this chapter, is Multiliteracies Pedagogy (New London Group, 1996, p. 63). *Multiliteracies* was coined by the New London Group (NLG) in a seminal article published in the Harvard Educational Review in 1996. The term "multiliteracies" immediately shifts us from the dominance of written, print text to acknowledge the complexities of practices, modes, technologies, and languages which literate people need to engage in the contemporary world.

The emphasis in Multiliteracies is on *multiple discourses*, *multiple designs*, and *multiple metalanguages* to support students and educators as they navigate through changes in their lives (Clark, 2007, p. 35). Cope and Kalantzis (2000) stress that there is nothing radically new in a multiliteracies pedagogy; prevailing pedagogy has simply been repackaged in order to expand the scope for literacy by viewing many types of expression and communication as literacies, whether formal or informal; spoken, gestured, written or graphic; official or unofficial (Ryan & Anstey, 2003).

The focus is on these competencies and digitally mediated literacy practices that students need to acquire and utilize in various contexts in order to succeed in the postmodern world. From the policy makers' and educators' perspective, a tension is present to incorporate these understandings in their practices to engage students in meaningful, relevant to life experiences that prepare them for a multicultural, multimedia-based world. Yet, contrary to this pervasive need, research has consistently shown that print literacy reading and writing activities still dominate mainstream learning contexts.

The goals and ideas of multiliteracies pedagogy require a holistic approach to schooling, one that I believe is better served when considering the theory proposed by Gee (2004) known as affinity spaces. Gee opposed a traditional schooling system that persists, promotes dominant discourses and hierarchies. He suggests instead an alternative view of schools.

Building on Jean Lave and Etienne Wenger's (1991) concept of *communities of practice* (thinking of groups of people as being either "in" or "out" of a community), Gee suggests that we think of spaces where people interact. An *affinity space* is a place—virtual or physical—where informal learning takes place. Spaces can be real tangible spaces, like a classroom, or virtual spaces, like an online discussion forum or game (Savva, 2016a). This shared space exists for people to interact and share their ideas based on common interests, endeavours, goals, or practices, without regard to race, gender, age, disability, or social class (Gee, 2004, p. 67). To think of it in practical terms, an example of affinity spaces is an online forum, an online game environment, etc., where users feel a sense of belonging and share common interests and feedback.

In discussing characteristics of what are considered to be *affinity spaces*, Gee and Hayes (2009) acknowledge how within this type of spaces, we do not distinguish between novices and experienced individuals, but rather we coexist. Affinity spaces, according to them, encourage users to gain both intensive (experts or specialists) and extensive (broad knowledge shared with everyone) knowledge, while also enable use of dispersed knowledge (available outside the affinity space) and tacit knowledge (knowledge built up in practice not able to express with words) (Gee & Hayes, 2009).

Learners or users of these spaces participate in varied ways and different levels, peripherally and centrally. Leadership is porous and leaders are resources. Different people lead in different days in different areas, and engage in resourcing, mentoring, and advising others (Gee & Hayes, 2009). Gee points out that schools do not have the features of affinity spaces, since distributed knowledge, networking, and collaboration across and beyond the school rarely occur. However, these are ways in which students interact and engage in their daily lives and should be incorporated into the school system (Morgan, 2010). Magnifico, Lammers, and Fields (2017) note the importance of user-generated affinity spaces as potentially useful for reinvigorating classroom practices and to expose students to learning opportunities for creation and critique.

The above concepts are touchstones in this exploration seeking to address the development of skills, but also the application of skills in changing situations and contexts as potential paths for educating knowmads. The MDAS framework offers an example of a creative synergy between the notion of affinity spaces and multiliteracies pedagogy to provide a teaching and learning approach that could apply to the goals and practices of a more suitable, knowmad-enabled, educational paradigm for our times. I next address the current situation in formal education and how this could change by viewing educators as learning architects within the MDAS framework.

The why

Formal education diachronically appears stiff to changes, and it reflects this in the obsolete mechanisms and practices still adopted in most educational systems around the world. This problematic nature is evident in the mismatches identified by Cobo in *Knowmad Society* and relate to a significant confusion: what knowledge implies. The elusive understanding of knowledge lies because as Moravec (2016a) puts it, we cannot measure a person's knowledge. Yet, deeply rooted in all educational systems until today, has been a mutual agreement that we can quantify knowledge, or else there will be "existential chaos." This *a priori* assumption has ramifications for the way education unfolds, its premises and promises, and its outcomes.

Through failing standardized instruction and testing, we fail ourselves as researchers and practitioners, and lead students to "fail" on a daily basis. However, the renowned entrepreneur Gary Vaynerchuck (2017) asserts, "I didn't fail school, school failed me. School fails entrepreneurs everyday because it's not built for entrepreneurs, it's built for workers." As Moravec (2016a) crucially questions, "What are we educating for?"

For the largest part of formal educational history, individuals are taught to become industrial workers and later information workers, crippled by any liberty to self-regulate their learning. However, it is now widely accepted that we need to educate for the next generation of leaders, innovators and creators – the knowmadic workers of the future. If we are to accept that a knowmad is able to learn and unlearn continuously anytime and anywhere (Moravec, 2008), we need to equip this person with all the skills necessary to be able to adapt in this mode of "invisible" learning.

Invisible learning, developed by Cobo and Moravec in their book *Aprendizaje invisible* (2011), refers to the shift of power to the learner, by trusting them first, and facilitating their self-directed learning thereafter, away from the traditional antiquated methods of authoritative teacher roles and rigid structures. This shift in paradigm should not come with a blindfold. Student learners, as Moravec (2016a) puts it in his theory of invisible learning, should be immersed in a genuine learning environment focused on context, and be encouraged to act as mold-breakers, be flexible to change and adapt in new environments and solve problems, and stay humble, while exhibiting self-determination.

Kalantzis, Cope, & Harvey (2003, p. 15) agree that effective learners should be autonomous and of open sensibility. This type of invisible learning, that is powerful and can promote change, is very different from the prevalent example of education and schooling. Current methods are unable to promote and measure effectively these skills and sensibilities (Kalantzis et al., 2003, p. 15).

The how

Rethinking pedagogy for the 21st century, as Scott (2015, p. 2) suggests, "is as crucial as identifying the new competencies that today's learners need to develop." It is undeniable that the new millennium has introduced new tools for communication and that educators determine the value of these tools and the effects on the curricula. It is therefore critical to question which pedagogies are appropriate for the 21st century and to what extent traditional approaches appeal to today's learner. What do we need to change and how feasible is it?

So far, attempts at a dramatic holistic transformation in education, and hence in school design, as futurist David Houle (2017) pointed out at the A4LE International Conference in Atlanta Indiana, are based on "current reform efforts [that] are reactionary and based on playing catch-up," and soon become obsolete. Confined by our persistence to stay loyal to an old paradigm, all those involved in learning, from theorists to practitioners, are often limited to old assumptions. Yet, to escape this "walled garden" of confinement, we should seek a more translucent approach to education through a new lens. Hartkamp (2013, p.140) stresses, "we [should] invent a new language" to consider education and schooling. To achieve this end, we should view educators as "learning architects" (Davenport, 2016). To better illustrate the identity of a learning architect, I suggest looking into the objectives this role serves first:

- To consider different ways to imagine education taking place in a post-classroom environment;
- To explore the trends that will affect the evolution of the educational environment;

- To ask new questions about a revolution in future educational systems and where they're heading; and,
- To stimulate interactions between experiences from different professions, geographical locations, and perspectives.

A *learning architect* is therefore a person who exhibits an understanding of good and next practices related to educational leadership, programming, teaching, learning, planning, and facility design. This individual should help schools create a clear vision, with a clearly defined roadmap, bringing together learning tools, platforms, and content into a form that is easy to use, scaling and delivering a great learner experience. Here, I argue that the best approach to achieve the latter is through re-conceptualizing the role of educators. Through my research, I have identified several overlapping roles which can inform the kind of educators we need for a knowmad society.

First, although the MDAS framework is not designed for teaching a specific curriculum or subject, educators in these premises should position themselves as *teachers of literacy*; yet this conception of literacy is broadened in functional terms of providing access to multimodal texts, the burgeoning textual forms such as interactive comics, videos, films, graphics, and visual images that students "read" (New London Group, 2000; Rowsell et al., 2008).

Second, the MDAS framework suggests that educators become critical readers of various forms of texts. Freire and Macedo name this role *teachers play as initiators of change* (1987). Ajayi (2011, p. 398) and Rowsell et al. (2008) argued that new communication technologies afford learners unlimited potential to practice multiple literacies across cultural, social, economic, and national boundaries. In the process, they re-conceptualize their self-identities as multiple, hybrid, complex, and dynamic beings.

Another significant role for an educator in the MDAS framework is to act not as an authority figure, the only possessor and transmitter of knowledge, but to become a *co-designer* or *co-inquirer* (Yayli, 2009, p. 207) of the social futures for learners, drawing from the concept of design found in multiliteracies pedagogy. In this sense, they would act as co-inquirers in meaning making. Educators take roles as researchers of knowledge. Any attempt to meet the challenges of the new communication landscape and enable educators and pupils to engage in new forms of literacy should pay attention to the role of teachers as *knowledge creators* in this endeavor (Farren, Keane, Hennessy & O'Mahony, 2007, p.1).

The above role is also supported by the notion of *teachers as border-crossers* (Giroux, 1992, p. 26), which emphasizes that teachers are learners who continuously develop themselves in their transitions from one sub-culture into another. This notion considers that teachers should become agents of *social inclusion* in teaching students whose cultural backgrounds differ from their own (Helfrich & Bean, 2011, p. 215).

From this point on, I connected each of the five trends proposed by Cobo in *Knowmad Society*, to explore how the MDAS framework nurtures the conditions necessary to ensure "multi-skilled profiles" and "multi-contextual learning practices" for an expanded understanding of education. These five trends are: 1) Informal and flexible learning approaches; 2) Lifelong, self-learning, and learning to learn; 3) ICT and critical thinking skills and new literacies; 4) Evolving conceptions of space-time and a lifelong learning environment (which is rarely time or context dependent); and, 5) The development of soft skills (global, tacit, and social).

1 Informal and flexible learning approaches

A basic premise in the description of a knowmad society (Society 3.0) and its function, is a distinction from previous forms of societies, namely the industrial society (Society 1.0), and information-based society (2.0). Moravec stresses how, "in the past, we applied for jobs. Now we are asked to design our work" (Moravec, 2013a, p. 19). In other words, the postmodern world, requires individuals to take up ownership of their learning and work, and to become inventors of their work.

Howard Gardner, as early as 1983, emphasized the need to explore more appropriate designs of educational systems to better suit the demands of the changing global economy. He introduced critical thinking skills, as essential to link school learning to the needs of the job market and to develop a strong workforce. In *Five minds for the future* (2006), Gardner revisits his original thoughts and argues how we will each need to master "five minds" that the fast-paced future will demand:

- The disciplinary mind, to learn at least one profession, as well as the major thinking philosophies behind it (science, math, history, etc.);
- The synthesizing mind, to organize the massive amounts of information and communicate effectively to others;
- The creating mind, to revel in unasked questions and uncover new phenomena and insightful answers;
- The respectful mind, to appreciate the differences between human beings and understand and work with all persons; and,
- The ethical mind, to fulfill one's responsibilities as both a worker and a citizen.

These suppositions are meaningful to instill understanding on the "multiskilled profiles" and "multi-contextual learning practices" of knowmadic workers. The fast-paced world in which we live in requires reconsidering the skills future job seekers should have, but also their adaptive capacity—the flexibility to adapt in diverse contexts and challenges—as individuals. This stems from a realization that each of us learns in different ways—our learning ecologies—at their own pace and time. It is therefore impossible to have a single approach to schooling that will serve all learners.

As Moravec (2016a) points out, society needs knowmadic workers who work with context, not within a rigid structure. McCoog (2008) suggests that educators have a new charge: teach *the new three Rs*: rigor, relevance, and real world skills. He captures the critical demands of contemporary societies by stressing that:

> *Today's students are acquiring 21st century skills, and what surprises teachers the most is that they are not the ones teaching them. 21st century learners have taught themselves to network and find solutions, which makes them expect to have the same experience at school. (McCoog, 2008, p. 1)*

Despite the proliferation of the term "21st century skills" over the past three decades, these have yet to be addressed holistically in education. The MDAS framework could provide a route towards informal and flexible learning approaches. The ultimate goal of literacy pedagogy in the MDAS framework should be to enable the reader to use any or all of the resources available, to transform the meaning of texts, to be meaningful to the reader, and applicable to different contexts, whether virtual or physical. Lave (1996, p. 161) refers to this as "changing participation in changing practices." We must teach students to recruit previous and current experiences as an integral part of learning to make meaning (Cope & Kalantzis, 2000).

In practical terms, learning in the MDAS framework draws on four core knowledge processes: experiencing, conceptualizing, analyzing, and applying. These are quality-driven aspects of the learning process firstly introduced by Kolb (1984) and Bernice McCarthy (1987) in their 4MAT model. The four ways of knowing have been expanded by Kalantzis and Cope (2005) in their Learning by Design Model (LbD)—among the authors of the manifesto on multiliteracies pedagogy—as a guideline to teach and learn in formal education.

Experiencing involves a personal engagement in sensations, emotions, physical memories, involvement of the self, and immersion in the world (human and natural). Conceptualizing is the translation and synthesis of experiences, conceptual forms, language, and symbols into abstract generalizations. Analyzing is the transformation of knowledge by ordering, reflecting on, and interpreting the underlying rationale for particular designs and representations. Applying is the experiential application of internal thought processes to external situations in the world by testing the world and adapting knowledge to multiple, ambiguous situations (Kalantzis & Cope, 2005, p. 96). These knowledge processes intend to enable teachers to analyze the learning that occurs when a pedagogy of multiliteracies is implemented, and promote critical skills, such as problem solving, reflection, creativity, critical thinking, learning to learn, risk-taking, collaboration, and entrepreneurship.

The mix of knowledge processes in the LbD model is of most relevance to the knowmad concept, as it allows different emphases and activity types as appropriate to students' different "learning orientations" (Kalantzis & Cope, 2005, p. 97). All the knowledge processes also change the direction of the knowledge flows and the balance of responsibility for learning toward a more active view of learning as engagement.

In this context, learner identities and subjectivities become more manifested. Learning is conceived as a journey, in a transformational (rather than static) view of diversity, in which neither the world nor the learner are quite the same as they were at the beginning by the time their journey finishes. Therefore, the intention in this framework of practice, is to cultivate the ground for students to develop a mindset that allows them to be flexible learners, adaptive to different contextual challenges, and therefore become better equipped to respond to multiple job demands.

2 Life-long, self-learning, and learning to learn

Influential theorist John Dewey (1916, p. 239), stated, "education is not preparation for life; education is life itself." Education is not a result, but rather a lifetime process that is ongoing, experiential, occurs in different environments, and includes communication and understanding to grow as an individual and collectively. It is widely concerned that we live in the era of lifelong, self-directed learning. However, this does not adequately permeate formal education policy. Cobo agrees with Richard Rowe that, in order to foster a society of lifelong learners, we must seek to identify "how to design successful solutions" (Cobo, 2013, p. 61).

A central focus in MDAS framework is learning how to learn. Learning is considered a process of constant meaning-making, during which learners continually reshape themselves. Meaning-making and any other semiotic activity are treated as "a matter of design" (New London Group, 1996, p. 73). Design is seen as a dynamic process, not governed by static rules (New London Group, 2000, p. 20). It is a process of subjective self-interest and transformation of existing representational resources—such as linguistic patterns, genres, dialects, registers, and discourses/ideologies, as well as nonlinguistic modalities—to achieve the individual's/designer's communicative and cultural purpose (Lam, 2009, p. 379).

The concept of design is helpful, for example, as we consider how immigrant teens draw upon various representational resources to (re)define their identities and relations to multiple localities and communities in the process of migration (Lam, 2009, p. 379). *Learning by design* builds into a curriculum an understanding that not every learner will bring the same experiences and interests to learning (Kalantzis & Cope, 2012), and acknowledging that every learner is not on the same page at the same time (Kalantzis & Cope, 2005). This is a fundamental principle within the MDAS framework.

Barton, Hamilton, & Ivanič (2000) speak of merging students' *schoolworlds* and *lifewords* to expand their repertoires of literacy. They identify these different domains or identities collectively as Discourse Worlds, and suggest that students draw on two in particular to make meaning, their lifeworld and their school-based world (Barton et al., 2000; Anstey & Bull, 2006, p. 34). These worlds overlap and inform one another. Part of readers' life-based worlds and school-based worlds is their knowledge and experience. The literature asserts that exposing students to experiences relevant to their lifeworlds and cultures can motivate them and provide them with opportunities to engage in the lesson in a more meaningful way (González, Moll & Amanti, 2005, p.6). In this type of sociocultural approach:

> *The focus of learning and education is not children, nor schools, but human lives viewed as trajectories through multiple social practices in various social institutions. (Gee, Hull & Lankshear, 1996, p. 4)*

Such situated practice presupposes a consideration of lifeworld-based learner diversity such as the multiple intelligences, identified by Gardner (2004) as linguistic, logical-mathematical, spatial, bodily kinesthetic, musical, naturalist, intrapersonal, and interpersonal. Most importantly, situated practice addresses the need to recognize the students' native languages, home languages, or first languages—especially if the languages are not the dominant language of the school. Key to facilitating this process is metalanguage.

Metalanguage represents the grammar of multiliteracies pedagogy; furthermore, it is used to explain patterns of meaning created during the design process. In a multiliteracies-influenced educational program, students draw on their experiences, interests and knowledge (available designs) and transform their processes (designing) into remade or new resources (redesigned) (New London Group, 1996, pp. 73-74). This way they become "active designers" (New London Group, 1996, p. 64) as self-directed learners who learn how to learn, with the help of experienced others (educators). The outcome of designing is the creation of new meaning. Others can then use the redesigned or transformed notions of meaning as available designs to draw upon for new outcomes (New London Group, 1996, 2000).

3 ICT and critical thinking skills and new literacies

Today's kids, as John Sealy Brown puts it, live and breathe ICTs (2002). They use technologies transparently (Jukes, 2005) and almost instinctively, without a safety net. In particular, for the "millennial generation" born after 1981 (Hagood, Stevens, & Reinking, 2002) reality includes new literacies embedded in these new technologies (Lankshear & Knobel, 2003). The exponential growth of emerging technologies has inevitably altered how we learn and also what it means to be literate.

Davies (2006) contends that although students are becoming increasingly literate multimodally, and although theories and testaments of multiliteracies have been established with increasing research evidence on their feasibility, schools remain focused on traditional print-bound modes and practices. Often new literacies are not part of policy documents, and if they occur, they remain isolated initiatives, supporting traditional literacy practices (Leu, Kinzer, Coiro, & Cammack, 2004). Dyson (2003) argued that there is a critical disconnect between the theory of multiliteracies and classroom pedagogy because "literacy development seldom includes any substantive consideration of such practices" (p. 330).

Moravec (2013b, p. 35) stresses the paradox of the co-existence of "Education 1.0" in "Society 3.0." *Society 3.0*, as he explains, refers to an emerging future that is characterized by accelerating technological and social change, continuing globalization, and horizontalization of knowledge and relationships, driven by knowmads working within an innovation society.

A critical factor for the effective incorporation of appropriate and creative blends between the digital and print literacies for young learners is the role of the educator (Miller, 2008). McGee (2007, p. 1) addresses this issue and explains that teachers are usually neither prepared or willing to engage students in any deconstruction of multimedia and multimodal texts, nor in the production of these texts. They often resist learning about new technologies or using them (IEAB, n.d). Educators must seek to repurpose the use of technologies to help students learn how to learn (Moravec, 2013b), to go beyond simplistic uses and applications, toward employing them as tools to co-create with peers, acting as learning hubs.

Notably, the challenge for educators is "not only to educate for new breadth and forms of literacy but also to have learners delve into a critical interpretation of these forms and modes" (Thwaites, 2003, p. 27). Individuals should consider different perspectives, analyze and problem-solve complex issues, and think critically about social issues. To succeed in the latter, it is important to bring students' prior experiences, knowledge, and interests into learning from the use of technologies, as these offer meaningful contexts for students' literacy learning. In the MDAS framework, learning occurs from incorporating all of these resources into challenging learning activities through addressing multimodality.

Kress refers to multimodality as a "domain of inquiry" (2009, p. 54), which discusses learners' movement between written, oral, visual, audio, tactile, gestural, and spatial modes, combined during communication to produce meaning (Kress & van Leeuwen, 1996). Multimodal literacy (Jewitt & Kress, 2003) emerged from the notion of multimodality. This view of literacy incorporates four types of skills. It encourages a range of language-based skills mediated through multimodal forms and representations; evaluative skills that could critically assess the nature, representational techniques, explicit, and subtle effects of exhibits; oral and presentation skills in communicating proposed plans and perspectives clearly and effectively; and, independent research skills used to source and adapt content from multiple sources for specific purposes (D'Acquisto, 2006).

Therefore, language learning becomes concrete through addressing the multiple dimensions of the multimodal design process (Jewitt, 2006). The aim of teaching literacy with respect to multimodality in the MDAS framework lies in the acquisition of abilities and skills necessary to produce various text forms linked with information and multimedia technologies (Baldry, 2000, p. 21). These multimodalities disrupt students' understandings and encourage learning. A knowmadic worker, is a multiliterate person who possesses a range of literacies, reads multimodal texts in an integrated fashion, and produces multimodal texts managing various resources (Kress, 1995).

4 The changing conceptions of space-time and lifelong learning environments (which are rarely time or context dependent);

A concept close to the release of control structures in education proposed by Moravec and Cobo in *Invisible learning*, is ubiquitous learning. Cope and Kalantzis (2008, p.576) suggest that "ubiquitous learning is a new educational paradigm." *Ubiquitous learning* relates to spaces of omnipresent learning where means of virtual and electronic resources are made available through portable devices (Peng, Chou, & Chang, 2008). This broadening of the *where* of learning is part of a greater movement towards 'lifelong learning' which, as discussed earlier, is a central feature of the present.

Cope and Kalantzis (2008) suggest that educational transformation is possible through certain 'moves' characteristic of ubiquitous learning. These include:

- Move 1: Learn at any place and anytime (remove institutional, spatial, and temporal boundaries);
- Move 2: Shift the balance of agency through a blurring of the boundaries between the teacher and the student;
- Move 3: Recognize learner differences and use them as a productive resource for work in groups;
- Move 4: Enable a greater range and mix of meanings in multiple ways, multimodally: the oral, the written, the visual, and the auditory;
- Move 5: Interact with multimodal texts using higher-order abstraction and metacognitive strategies;
- Move 6: Learn how to learn through renewed approaches for teaching and learning; and,
- Move 7: Address learner differences in terms of "experience, knowledge, ways of thinking and ways of seeing" (Cope & Kalantzis, 2008, p. 581) through building collaborative knowledge cultures.

The MDAS framework could inform the practical implementation of this approach to learning through addressing each of these aspects. Acting as an ecosystem of dynamic affinity spaces, it enables ubiquitous learning by a blurring of boundaries between the real and virtual through technology-enhanced means. The intention is to sharpen the processes of inquiry and

Table 5. Questions across five dimensions to describe meaning.

Dimension	Question to add depth to meaning
Representational	What do meanings refer to?
Social	How do meanings connect the persons they involve?
Organizational	How do the meanings hang together?
Contextual	How do the meanings fit into the larger world of meaning?
Ideological	Whose interests are the meanings skewed to serve?

Note. Adapted from Cope & Kalantzis (2000, pp. 212-217).

learning through a critical engagement with these multimodal ways and resources. A central goal is to enhance participant collaboration and exchange through addressing and using students' cultural diversity and their different backgrounds in the learning process.

To infuse these approaches as part of the designing process in the MDAS framework, learners redesign their available resources so they can remake meaning: transfer learning to other contexts, recreate their designs for meaning-making, and implement their newly-created designs for learning. Cope and Kalantzis (2000, p. 65) suggest an examination of five dimensions of meaning (representational, social, organizational, contextual, and ideological) across six modes of meaning (linguistic, visual, gestural, spatial, audio, and multimodal) to support teachers in their endeavors to describe the interplay and integration of modes of meaning (Table 5).The effect of the design process in the MDAS framework is to expand students' cultural and representational understandings beyond where they already are, in seeking to promote deeper forms of knowing and meaning. Students' knowledge is the foundation on which educators build to further students' understandings in various, meaningful contexts, unconfined by virtual or physical limitations. The intention in such an approach is dual: for students to show growth in content areas and personal growth, while they reconstruct and negotiate their identities within the multiple discourses at play.

5 The development of soft skills (global, tacit, and social)

Hal Gregersen, Clayton Christensen, and Jeff Dyer, in their book, The *Innovator's DNA: Mastering the five skills of disruptive innovators* (2011), ask a significant question: "Is an innovator born or made?" They conclude that individuals can develop the skills necessary to move progressively from idea to impact, leading to disruptive innovation. Our ability to generate innovative ideas is not just a function of our minds, but of our behaviors. It can be taught. They identify five distinct 'discovery skills' of disruptive innovators:

- Questioning: Posing queries that challenge common wisdom;
- Observing: Scrutinizing the behavior of customers, suppliers, and competitors to identify new ways of doing things;
- Networking: Meeting people with different ideas and perspectives;
- Experimenting: Constructing interactive experiences and provoking unorthodox responses to see what insights emerge; and,
- Associating: Making connections between questions, problems, or ideas from unrelated fields.

Essentially, Gergersen et al. (2011) maintain that we can build our Innovator's DNA through cultivating a culture and capabilities for innovation. This mindset, instilled as a culture of innovating, is crucial for determining the prerequisites for educating knowmadic workers. Despite a rapid expansion of higher education institutions across Europe in the last three decades, together with an increasing number of qualified candidates available in the job market, graduate employability is doubtful.

There is an evident gap identified between the skills and capabilities of graduates, and the demands and requirements of the work environment in our complex globalized society (Andrews & Higson, 2008). The quality of the graduate labor market and the ability of graduates to meet the needs of employers directly relate to the skills promoted in higher education institutions.

Employers and higher education professors frequently complain of a lack of soft skills among tertiary education graduates. This derives partly from the persistence in an obsolete paradigm for education, focused on quantifiable results related to functional, technical skills pertaining to rigid forms of prefabricated goals for knowledge attainment. Soft skills relate to attributes/

traits that are rather difficult to measure and relate to the development of thinking minds like knowmads, and thus are often overlooked in formal educational settings. Dede (2010), as Cobo notes in *Knowmad Society*, acknowledges a platform of key soft skills that inform educational frameworks, including critical thinking, searching, synthesizing and disseminating information, creativity and innovation skills, collaboration skills, contextual learning skills, self-direction, and communication skills.

Lievens & Chan (2017), assert that innovation stems from both soft and hard skills (tangible, functional skills needed for a job). Increasing evidence suggests that the two sets of skills are complementary. Although there is not a consensus of what we mean by *soft skills*, it appears that they derive from practical intelligence, social intelligence, and emotional intelligence. Lievens and Chan (2017), maintain that these constructs of intelligence share remarkable similarities. They suggest viewing the three in an integrated framework where they exist as inherently multidimensional constructs, unique but overlapping.

The philosophy manifested in the MDAS framework nurtures the development of global, tacit, and social skills naturally, through practice and understanding. There is increasing evidence from research on engagement with multiliteracies, that show how students benefit in terms of an array of soft skills. For example, in my doctoral investigation into affinity multiliteracies learning spaces, students engaged in the development of a student generated virtual museum environment, which acted as a user-generated affinity space. Taking up a design-based research, my study enquired specifically into approaches to design, implement and evaluate a museum-school partnership for the 21st-century, through adhering to the unique characteristics of virtual museum environments and their potential for multimodal engagement and learning. The focus was on the experiences of 4 schoolteachers, 2 museum educators and 36 primary students aged 10-12 years old, in the island of Cyprus. The intention was to examine culturally and linguistically diverse students' repertoires of literacy as they engaged in the learning process, taking the roles of active designers and multimodal learners. Towards this end, the evaluation was derived from cognitive, interpersonal, group, resource, and institutional level criteria (Savva, 2019), proposed by Collins et al. (2004).

Findings showed that this learning environment enabled a dynamic student role (Savva & Souleles, 2014). Students directed their own investigatory activities. They were actively involved in asking questions, creatively planned their activities, and reached to conclusions about their work. Interacting within the premises of an affinity space also served to fulfil some aspects of culturally-responsive learning. The students believed they were reintroduced to the school environment starting from a clean sheet when they engaged in this project (Savva & Souleles, 2014).

Magnifico et al. (2017) assert that affinity spaces value diverse participation and can lead to deeper learning. For students to be deeply engaged in tasks that enable higher-order skills, they require passionate, positive feelings about these tasks. Engagement occurs when the cognitive, the affective, and the operative occur together at a high level (Fair Go Team, 2006, p. 10).

Students in my research gained confidence through interacting with their peers online, while also demonstrating personal self-esteem and good social organization skills. I employed *Webquests*, an active process of directed discovery during which students take up an active role to solve a problem or participate in a realistic situation (Dodge, 1999). This inquiry-driven process supported students' analytical and higher order thinking skills and encouraged them to interpret the social context and purpose of designs of meaning (New London Group, 1996) through direct involvement in analyzing purposes, comparing, commenting on, discussing consequences, and evaluating concepts.

The most difficult and higher-order form of competence in the MDAS framework relates to collaborative thinking, as it involves communication, negotiation, and sensitivity apart from solid subject matter knowledge (Savva, 2016a). Findings from this interpersonal aspect of the evaluation of the partnership indicated that students appeared to benefit from the collaborative learning dimension (Kuhn et al., 2000; Vygotsky, 1978).

Within the affinity space cultivated, collaborative learning flourished as students learned to identify problems collaboratively with peers via observation and dialogue, inference, form, and testing (Savva, 2016b). They seemed to benefit and appreciate this scaffolding and support of the project, which allowed them to improve both by learning on their own but also while learning with others in the group (Looi et al., 2010).

Giving and receiving feedback in these extracurricular and blended affinity spaces helps maintain a higher level of interest as individuals become more aware of their own competence (e.g., Lipstein & Renninger, 2007). In this sense, students became designers of their experiences while working in groups as collaborative knowledge producers (Cope & Kalantzis, 2008, p. 581). Kafai and Burke (2014) suggest shifting beyond "computational thinking" to "computational participation" in considering the different roles that end-users and online communities play. It is important to acknowledge the variant participation styles present in creative, online affinity spaces, and how these styles can inform teachers' efforts to connect existing curricula with online spaces (Magnifico et al., 2017).

Concluding remarks: Shaping a knowmad society

The present educational landscape is one where top-down, test-driven strategies and primarily print-based literacies prevail. Most alternative initiatives are sporadic and soon become obsolete. As adeptly stated in *Manifesto 15*, "1.0 schools cannot teach 3.0 kids" (Moravec, 2016b, p. 4)." Only when we reconfigure the settings of what we are educating for, why we do it, and for whom our educational systems serve, it will be feasible to truly transform education futures (Moravec, 2016b, p. 4).

The key to creating for a knowmad-enabled educational paradigm, is found in bridging the gap between schoolworld and lifeworld experiences. Fabricating stories is not adequate for individuals to learn; they need to be co-creators and co-designers of their learning experiences; the environmental context is imperative to learning, and as the MDAS framework suggests, teachers should strive to provide authentic, real-world experiences and problems which are relevant to students and their backgrounds and interests. I suggest that it can become meaningful in a discussion of a formal theory for invisible learning and for the conditions that enable the education of knowmads.

- Teachers and facilitators should recognize the enormity of social change in today's classrooms. Students bring into the classroom and the museum a complex range of representational resources based on diverse cultures in their lived experiences (Cope & Kalantzis, 2000).
- Literacy learning is situated in the social and cultural practices of students and is distributed across their peers, contexts, and technologies (Gee, 2003).
- Skills are broadly configured and situated in specific contexts that shape understanding. The aim should be co-construction of knowledge and opportunities for authentic engagement and participation, drawing on the identities, agency, and everyday practices of pupils.
- Meaning making requires attention to a wide variety of media and diverse modes of representation. These should be integrated into school practice for students to analyze, critically interpret, and transform for application in new contexts.
- Multiliteracies pedagogy offers the potential to deploy pluralism, linguistic diversity, and cross-cultural synergy through introducing multimodal educational resources.
- Multiliteracies pedagogy recognizes differences and meshes students' differing interests, priorities, and needs. Attendant languages, hybrid cross cultural discourses, cross-cultural dialects, intertextuality, and regional dialects server as resources for teaching and learning.
- A multiliteracies-driven curriculum and schooling could facilitate the realization of a knowmadic society as a site of negotiation, contestation, interpretation, and reconfiguration of relationships of alternative frame-works and mindsets.

In the MDAS framework, the focus is on the student. Such self-driven, ubiquitous learning occurs synchronously and asynchronously, unconfined by time and space limitations in a reinvigorating balancing act of letting go, following up from students' interests and topics of interest. Having implemented the MDAS framework in multiple settings, including a school, a museum, and an art gallery, I believe it is entirely feasible to draw on students' interests and address their needs, while enabling them to question and critically analyze existing understandings. This can allow them to reach to a level of metalanguage that transforms practice depending on the context.

A basic precondition for MDAS to be successful though, is the willingness of the teachers to learn and unlearn, to continually challenge ourselves as educators, and be ready to release ourselves from our bird box. Only then, we may create personally-meaningful value in students' learning (Moravec, 2013b).

The future belongs to nerds, geeks, makers, dreamers and innovative thinkers (Moravec, 2013b) at large; it belongs to knowmads. All relevant bodies that care for the development of multi-skilled learners in multi-contextual practices can be beneficiaries of the MDAS framework, a knowledge-enabled approach to educate in the Knowmad Society.

REFERENCES

Ajayi, L. (2011). A multiliteracies pedagogy: Exploring semiotic possibilities of a Disney video in a third grade diverse classroom. *Urban Rev, 43*, 396–413.

Andrews, J., & Higson, H. (2008). Graduate employability, 'soft skills' versus 'hard' business knowledge: A European study, *Higher Education in Europe, 33*(4), 411-422, doi:10.1080/03797720802522627

Anstey, M., & Bull, G. (2006). *Teaching and learning multiliteracies.* Delaware: International Reading Association.

Baldry, A.P. (2000). Introduction. In Baldry, A. (Ed.), *Multimodality and multimediality in the distance learning age* (p. 11). Campobasso, Italy: Palladino.

Barton, D., Hamilton, M., & Ivanič, R. (eds.) (2000) *Situated literacies: Reading and writing in context.* London: Routledge.

Brown, J.S. (2002). Learning in the Digital Age. In M. Devlin, R. Larson & J. Meyerson (eds.), *The Internet & the university: Forum 2001* (pp. 65-91). Published as a joint project of the Forum for the Future of Higher Education and EDUCAUSE.

Clark, K.R. (2007). *Charting transformative practice: Critical multiliteracies via informal learning design.* UC San Diego Electronic Theses and Dissertations.

Cobo, C. (2013). Skills and competencies for knowmadic workers. In Moravec, J.W. (Ed.), *Knowmad Society* (pp. 57-88). Minneapolis: Education Futures.

Cobo, C., & Moravec, J.W. (2011). *Aprendizaje Invisible: Hacia una nueva ecología de la educación.* Barcelona: Laboratori de Mitjans Interactius / Publicacions i Edicions de la Universitat de Barcelona.

Collins, A.M., Joseph, D., & Bielaczyc, K. (2004). Design research: Theoretical and methodological issues, *Journal of the Learning Sciences, 13*(1), 15–42.

Cope, B., & Kalantzis, M. (2000). *Multiliteracies: Literacy learning and the design of social futures.* South Yarra: Macmillan.

Cope, B., & Kalantzis, M. (2008). Ubiquitous learning: An agenda for educational transformation. *Proceedings of the 6th International Conference on Networked Learning*, Halkidiki, Greece, 576 – 582.

D'Acquisto, L. (2006). *Learning on display: Student-created museums that build understanding.* Alexandria, VA: Association for Supervision and Curriculum Development.

Davenport, T. (2016). *Instructional designer to learning architect: How learning – and how your role – is changing.* www.linkedin. com/pulse/from-instructional-designer-learning-architect-how-your-davenport/

Davies, J. (2006). "Hello newbie! **big welcome hugs** hope u like it here as much as i do!" An exploration of teenagers' informal online learning. In D. Buckingham & R. Willett (Eds.), *Digital generations: Children, young people, and new media* (pp. 211–228). Mahwah, NJ: Erlbaum.

Dede, C. (2010). Comparing frameworks for 21st century skills. In J. Bellanca & R. Brandt (eds.), *21st century skills: Rethinking how students learn* (pp. 51–76). Bloomington, IN: Solution Tree.

Dewey, J. (1980). An added note as to the "practical." In J. A. Boydston (Ed.), *John Dewey: The middle works, 1899-1924* (pp. 366– 369). Carbondale, IL: Southern Illinois University Press. (Original work published 1916).

Dodge, B. (1999) *Some thoughts about WebQuests.* San Diego State University. Retrieved from webquest.sdsu.edu/about_webquests.html

Dyson, A.H. (2003). Welcome to the jam: Popular culture, school literacy, and the making of childhoods. *Harvard Educational Review, 73*(3), 328-362.

Fair Go Team NSW Department of Education and Training. (2006). *School is for me: Pathways to student engagement.* Sydney: NSW Department of Education and Training.

Farren, M., Keane, J., Hennessy, T., & O'Mahony, D. (2007). Teachers as knowledge creators. *CESI Conference 2007*, 16-17 Feb 2007, Dublin.

Fleming, D. (2005). Managing change in museums, *The museum and change International Conference*, 8-10 November 2005. National Museum, Prague, Czech Republic.

Freire, P., & Macedo, D. (1987). *Literacy: Reading the word and the world.* South Hadley, MA: Bergin & Garvey.

Gardner, D. P. (1983). *A nation at risk: The imperative for educational reform.* Washington, DC: US Government Printing Office.

Gardner, H. (2004). Audiences for the Theory of Multiple Intelligences. *Teachers College Record, 106*(1), 212-220.

Gardner, H. (2006). *Five minds for the future.* Boston, MA: Harvard Business School.

Gee, J.P. (2003). *What video games have to teach us about literacy and learning.* New York: Palgraw Macmillan.

Gee, J.P. (2004). *Situated language and learning: A critique of traditional schooling.* New York: Routledge.

Gee, J.P., & Hayes, E. (2009). Public pedagogy through video games: Design, resources & affinity spaces. *Game Based Learning.* www.gamebasedlearning.org.uk/content/view/59/

Gee, J.P., Hull, G., & Lankshear, C. (1996). *The new work order: Behind the language of the new capitalism.* St Leonards, NSW: Allen and Unwin.

Gregersen, H., Christensen, C. & Dyer, J. (2011). *The innovator's DNA: Mastering the five skills of disruptive innovators.* Brighton, MA: Harvard Business.

Giroux, H. (1992). *Border crossings: Cultural workers and the politics of education.* London: Routledge.

González, N., Moll, L.C., & Amanti, C. (Eds.). (2005). *Funds of knowledge: Theorizing practices in households, communities and classrooms.* Mahwah, NJ: Lawrence Erlbaum.

Hagood, M.C., Stevens, L.P., & Reinking, D. (2002). What do THEY have to teach US? Talkin' 'cross generations! In D.E. Alvermann (Ed.), *Adolescents and literacies in digital world.* New York: Peter Lang.

Hartkamp, C. (2013). Sudbury schools and democratic education. In Moravec, W. J. (ed.) K*nowmad Society* (pp. 129-162). Minneapolis: Education Futures.

Helfrich, S., & Bean, R. (2011). Beginning teachers reflect on their experiences being prepared to teach literacy. *Teacher Education and Practice, 24*(2), 201 - 222.

Houle, D. (2017). Keynote speech. *A4LE International Conference October 25-31, 2017,* Atlanta, GA.

International Education Advisory Board. (2006). *Learning in the 21st century: Teaching today's students on their terms.* www.certiport.com/Portal/ Common/ DocumentLibrary/IEAB_ Whitepaper040808.pdf

Jewitt, C. (2008). Multimodality and literacy in school classrooms. *Review of Research in Education, 1*, 241–267.

Jewitt, C., & Kress, G. (Eds.). (2003). *Multimodal literacy.* New York: Peter Lang.

Jukes, I. (2005) Understanding digital kids (DKs). *Teaching and learning in the new digital landscape.* The InfoSavvy Group.

Kalantzis, M., & Cope, B. (Eds.). (2005). *Learning by design.* Melbourne: Victorian Schools Innovation Commission and Common Ground.

Kalantzis, M., & Cope, B. (2012). *Literacies.* Cambridge, UK: Cambridge University Press.

Kalantzis, M., Cope, B., & Harvey, A. (2003). Assessing multiliteracies and the new basics. *Assessment in Education, 10*(1), 15-26.

Kolb, D.A. (1984). *Experiential learning: Experience as the source of learning and development.* New Jersey: Prentice-Hall.

Kress, G. (1995). *Writing the future: English and the making of a culture of innovation.* Sheffield: National Association for the Teaching of English.

Kress, G. (2009). *Multimodality: A social semiotic approach to contemporary communication.* New York: Routledge.

Kress, G., & Van Leeuwen, T. (Eds.). (1996). *Reading images: The grammar of visual design.* New York: Routledge.

Lankshear, C., & Knobel, M. (2006). *New literacies: Everyday practices and classroom learning.* New York: Open University Press.

Lam, W. (2009). Multiliteracies on instant messaging in negotiating local, translocal, and transnational affiliations: A case of an adolescent immigrant. *Reading Research Quarterly, 44*(4), 377–97.

Lave, J. (1996). Teaching as learning in practice. *Mind, Culture and Activity, 3*(3), 149-164.

Lave, J., & Wenger, E. (1991). *Situated learning. Legitimate peripheral participation.* Cambridge: Cambridge University Press.

Leu Jr., D.J., Kinzer, C.K., Coiro, J., & Cammack, D. (2004). Toward a theory of new literacies emerging from the Internet and other ICT. In R.B. Ruddell & N. Unrau (Eds.), *Theoretical models and processes of reading,* Fifth Edition (pp. 1568-1611). Newark, DE: International Reading Association.

Liddicoat, A. (2007). *Language planning and policy: Issues in language planning and literacy.* UK: Cromwell Press.

Lievens, F.R O., & Chan, D. (2017). Practical intelligence, emotional intelligence, and social intelligence. In In J.L.:Farr & N.T. Tippins (Eds.), *Handbook of employee selection* (pp. 342-364). New York: Routledge.

Lipstein, R.L., & Renninger, K.A. (2007). Putting things into words: the development of 12–15-year-old students' interest for Writing. In P. Boscolo, S. Hidi (Eds.), *Writing and motivation* (pp. 113–140). Oxford, UK: Elsevier.

Looi, C.K., Chen, W., & Ng, F.K. (2010). Collaborative activities enabled by Group Scribbles (GS): An exploratory study of learning effectiveness. *Computers and Education, 54*(1), 14–26.

Luke, A., & Freebody, P. (2000). *Literate futures: Report of the Literacy Review for Queensland State Schools,* Queensland Government Printer, Brisbane.

Magnifico, A.M., Lammers, J.C., & Fields, D.A. (2017). Affinity spaces, literacies and classrooms: tensions and opportunities. *Literacy, 52*(3), 145-152.

McCarthy, L.P. (1987). A stranger in strange lands: A college student writing across the curriculum. *RTE*, *21*(3), 233-265.

McCoog, I. (2008). *21st Century teaching and learning*. www.eric.ed.gov/ERICWebPortal/recordDetail?accno=E D502607

McGee, L.M. (2007). *Transforming literacy practices in preschool: Research-based practices that give all children the opportunity to reach their potential as learners*. New York: Scholastic.

Miller, S.M. (2008). Teacher learning for new times: Repurposing new multimodal literacies and digital-video composing for schools. In J. Flood, S.B. Heath & D. Lapp (Eds.), *Handbook of research on teaching literacy through the communicative and visual arts*. (pp. 441-460). New York: Lawrence Erlbaum Associates and the International Reading Association.

Montgomery, A., & Kehoe, I. (Eds.). (2016). *Reimagining the purpose of schools and educational organizations: Developing critical thinking, agency, beliefs in schools and educational organizations*. Cham, Switzerland: Springer.

Moravec, J.W. (2008). A new paradigm of knowledge production in higher education. *On the Horizon, 16*(3), 123-136. doi: 10.1108/10748120810901422

Moravec, J.W. (ed.) (2013a). *Knowmad Society*. Minneapolis: Education Futures.

Moravec, J.W. (2013b). Rethinking human capital development. In Moravec, J.W. (Ed.), *Knowmad Society* (pp.31-56). Minneapolis: Education Futures.

Moravec, J.W. (2016a). A theory for invisible learning. *Education Futures*. educationfutures.com/blog/post/theory-invisible-learning

Moravec J.W. et al. (2016b). *Manifesto 15: Evolving learning. A handbook for leading change*. Minneapolis: Education Futures.

Morgan, L. (2010). Teacher professional transformation using learning by design: A case study. *E-Learning and Digital Media, 7*(3), 280–292.

New London Group. (1996). A pedagogy of multiliteracies: Designing social futures. *Harvard Educational Review, 66*(1), 60-92.

New London Group. (2000). A pedagogy of multiliteracies: Designing social futures. In B. Cope & M. Kalantzis (Eds), *Multiliteracies: Literacy learning and the design of social futures* (pp.182-202). Melbourne: Macmillan.

Peng, H., Chou, C., & Chang, C.-Y. (2008). From virtual environments to physical environments: Exploring interactivity in ubiquitous-learning systems. *Educational Technology & Society, 11*(2), 54–66.

Rowsell, J., Kosnik, C., & Beck, C. (2008). Fostering multiliteracies pedagogy through preservice teacher education. *Teaching Education, 19* (2), 109–122.

Ryan, M.E., & Anstey, M. (2003). Identity and text: Developing self-conscious readers. *Australian Journal of Language and Literacy, 26*(1), 9–22.

Savva, S. (2016a). *The potential of a museum-school partnership to support diversity and multiliteracies-based pedagogy for the 21st century*. Unpublished PhD thesis, University of Leicester, UK.

Savva, S. (2016b). Re-imagining schooling: weaving the picture of school as an affinity space for 21st century through a multiliteracies lens. In A. Montgomery & I. Kehoe. (Eds.), *Reimagining the purpose of schools and educational organisations*, Netherlands: Springer Publishing.

Savva, S. (2019). Emergent digital multiliteracy practices at the core of the museum-school partnership. In T. Cerratto-Pargman & I. Jahnke (Eds.), *Emergent practices and material conditions in learning and teaching with technologies*. Springer Publishing.

Savva, S. & Souleles, N. (2014). Using WebQuests in a multimodally dynamic virtual learning intervention: Ubiquitous learning made possible? *Ubiquitous Learning: An International Journal, 6*(3), 15-33.

Scott, C.L. (2015). The futures of learning 3: What kind of pedagogies for the 21st century? *Education Research and Foresight, Working Papers*. Paris: UNESCO.

Thwaites, T. (2003). Multiliteracies: A new paradigm for arts education. *ACE papers 2003, 13*, 14-29.

Vaynerchuck, G. (2017). School is failing entrepreneurs every day. youtu.be/PelOG3Ji1xk

Yayli, D. (2009). New roles for literacy teachers in the age of multiliteracies: A sociocultural perspective. *Procedia Social and Behavioural Sciences, 1*, 206–209.

Stefania Savva is a postdoctoral research fellow at the Cyprus University of Technology, awarded funding for her project Museum *Affinity Spaces (MAS): Re-imagining Museum-School Partnerships for the 21st century through a Multiliteracies Lens*. She has completed a PhD in Museum Studies at the University of Leicester, UK in 2016.

stefania.savva@cut.ac.cy

notes

Notes

notes

Reimagining teacher training: Building an innovative pathway from the lifelong learning and knowmad professional profiles

GABRIELA CARREÑO MURILLO

"Would you tell me, please, which way I ought to walk from here?"

"That depends a good deal on where you want to get to," said the Cat.

"I don't much care where—" said Alice.

"Then it doesn't matter which way you walk," said the Cat.

"—so long as I get somewhere," Alice added as an explanation.

"Oh, you're sure to do that," said the Cat, "if you only walk long enough."

Excerpt from *Alice's adventures in Wonderland*

by Lewis Carroll (2000, pp. 89-90)

Between uncertainty and social change in 21st century education.

As the cat answered Alice, the path to choose depends on where we want to go. And, with education, the obligatory questions are: Where do we want to go with current education? For what and why do we want to get there? What futures for education do we want to build? Are we doing it in the right way? Does the educational path that we have traveled so far allow students to be self-managing and autonomous in their learning? Does it allow students to apply their knowledge innovatively?

> *These issues apply to current education, just as Alice entered that amazing country of Wonderland, finding herself in complex and changing spaces and events: "How puzzling all these changes are! I'm never sure what I'm going to be, from one minute to another!" (Carroll, 2000, p. 74).*

This uncertain world for Alice is very similar to our current realities. We are, from the point of view of Galeano (2005) in an upside-down world:

> *One hundred and thirty years ago, after visiting Wonderland, Alice went into a mirror to discover the world upside down. If Alice were reborn in our days, she would not need to go through any mirror: it would be enough to lean out the window. At the end of the millennium, the world upside down is in sight: it is the world as it is, with the left to the right, the navel in the back and the head in the feet. (p.7)*

This upside-down world is incongruous, contradictory, and complex, but it does not carry a negative connotation. Because the present and the future are not linear, it does not have a sequence. Order and disorder dynamically coexist: the one and the multiple, the simple and the complex, the singular and the general, organization and disorganization, invariance and change, balance and imbalance, stability and instability, and the improbable and the probable (González, 2009).

These issues are closely linked to educational processes. Besides asking us which road or paths to travel to achieve the education we want, a second challenge lies in how to cope with changes, contradictions, high levels of complexity, and the natural relationship between order and disorder of "education."

Education, teaching, and learning, are not pure, passive, limited, or immutable forms. These elements make innovation, creation, and transformation possible. According to Morin, organizations have this need for order and disorder that drives them towards evolution and constant growth (Morin, 1990).

From this rationale of complexity, it is possible to understand why the teaching profession associates with routine elements, constants, order, and repetition; but also with elements of invariability, disorder, randomness, irregularity, deviation, and unpredictability. Barrera (2016) wrote that both elements, order and disorder, are indispensable in mainstream educational systems. This is because the classroom requires freedom and autonomy—with purpose and order. In educational spaces, it is necessary to experiment, discover things, generate knowledge, and connect with other people.

Besides the mutable and chaotic character of education, we must rethink the social, cultural, economic, and technological transformations that reconfigure the new educational scenarios of the 21st century. Cobo & Moravec (2011) refer to *Society 3.0*, which points to a world that transcends the avant garde, and is driven by three main trends:

- Accelerating social and technological change;
- Continuous globalization and horizontal redistribution of knowledge and relationships; and,
- An innovation society, driven by *knowmads*.

Continuing globalization is leading to a horizontalized diffusion of knowledge in domains that were previously siloed, creating heterarchical relation- ships, and providing new opportunities for knowledge to be applied contextually in innovative applications. In the realm of teaching and learning, this means that we are becoming not only co-learners, but also co-teachers as we co-constructively produce new knowledge and new applications for our knowledge. (Moravec, 2013, p. 39)

Considering these reconfigurations of scenarios, it is possible to understand why such concepts as a career, education, learning, teaching, employment, and training have transformed. Educating today is more complex than it seems and these contexts of change and uncertainty demand successive efforts to transform teachers' daily work often and in different contexts (Esteve, 2006).

It is therefore necessary to re-think and re-imagine work of teaching while considering all the previous scenarios, while defining a clear and focused path that responds to these challenges from a different understanding. This must in align with the complex nature of education, thus overcoming a simplistic, reductionist vision.

Teacher training and transformation

We are immersed in a period of *intra-generational* change, which makes us witnesses and protagonists in a world that more rapidly changes throughout our lifetimes and forces us to adapt to a multitude of situations. This generalized acceleration demands successive efforts of change in the daily work of educators. It is not only about accepting the change of a certain educational reform, but about accepting that social change will oblige us to transform our professional work several times throughout our professional life; or, more specifically, that teachers need to accept social change as a basic element to succeed in their work (Esteve, 2003).

There is strong evidence that the quality of teachers' ability to teach is a variable that most affects the quality of student learning. (Esteve, 1994;

Nóvoa 2009). In-service training programs focus on the needs of the school establishment, strengthen the quality, the teamwork and the institutional academic culture. (Tedesco & Tenti 2002). But, how to achieve all the above? Per Vaillant (2005), change and educational improvement may not be managed top-down and cannot be prescribed or implemented from decision spaces outside the school community.

Transforming teacher professional development must involve a systemic, integrated, and multidimensional change that recognizes the levels of complexity of education and the teaching profession itself. The interaction of different realities and personal, social, cultural, and institutional contexts create complexity. Hence, it is necessary to rethink, reorient, reimagine, and transform teacher training and lifelong learning through processes of diagnosis, reflection, innovation, self-management, disruption, and academic transformation.

Transformations adjust any internal or external training actions to the real demands of the teaching profession, starting not only from an imaginary teacher, but by a real teacher immersed in different scenarios and experiences. A comprehensive approach and a series of actions that generate scenarios of teacher training and development provide an opportunity for teachers to identify their areas of opportunity to continue learning and to improve their teaching styles.

Freire (1998), states that an educator's capability to educate is verified to the extent that she or he is permanently available to rethink what they previously thought and review their positions. This includes seeking to get involved with the curiosity of students and the different roads and paths that they have to travel.

New scenarios of teacher unlearning and learning

Being a teacher has become a complex practice, intersected by different spaces of formal, informal, and non-formal learning. It also requires something more than the mastery and the use of specialized, technical knowledge (Esteve, 1994). Freire, in *Letters for those who intend to teach* (1998), showed us how this critical meaning and requirement of teaching and learning is developed by affirming that the act of teaching requires the co-existence of the teacher and the learner because teaching does not exist without learning. It is necessary to adopt a much broader perspective of education, learning, and teaching, which accounts for the dynamic and conflicting nature of these processes.

> *I mean that teaching and learning are given in such a way that, on one hand, a person who teaches learns because they recognize previously learned knowledge, and, on the other hand, because observing how the learner's curiosity works to apprehend what is learned. He is teaching him, without which he does not learn, the educator helps himself to discover doubts, successes and mistakes (Freire, 1998, p. 28).*

The teacher as a critical-reflective professional

It is necessary to rethink the teachers themselves, placing them as active, reflective professionals and as allowed subjects in the production of their knowledge and pedagogical actions: (Richert, 2005). Professionals who face challenges and problems, who can think with others and seek expert knowledge allows them to overcome interventions in their classrooms and schools (Lombardi 1998). From this anchoring, it is possible to promote reflections, restructuring, and conceptualizations which open new scenarios of training and enable the transformation of teaching practice.

Educators' professional trajectories signify a construction that emerges from the interaction of multiple elements: contexts of academic activities; initial and continuous training; initial motivations and the future expectations of development, thought and action; and previous work routes. In this same sense, Fernandez affirms that teacher professionalization passes not only due to cognitive dimensions or teacher's techniques but also because of the other immense set of variables that refer to the world of attitudes, perceptions, personal choices of self-realization, personal satisfaction, labor, and affectivity (Fernández, 1995).

This personal, academic and professional development of teachers has expanded their learning and teaching scenarios, including all their previous experiences and the critical analysis of their daily practice. As Freire (1997) points out, there is always something different to do in one's daily educational life and it is by thinking critically about the practice of today or yesterday that we can improve the next practice.

Teacher learning as a spiral process

From this critical perspective, learning is not an end. It is a permanent process where the student learns, unlearns, and relearns in such a way that the learned object has several edges and ways of being thought, appropriately reflecting within its complex essence. Unlearning, Relearning, Learning and Complexing of an object or process (PDRAC) is not a simple, linear and unique process. Learning must lead to the complexity of the object to be learned (González, 2009). Hence, the key to this unlearning process lies in how you learn, not in what you learn (Cobo & Moravec, 2011, p. 61).

In this tenet proposed by Moravec, we can point out that teachers learn in a similar way as their students do: studying, doing, and reflecting; collaborating with other teachers; observing the students, their work, and sharing what they observe, what they analyze (Darling, 2001, p. 191).

People, including teachers, learn best when they make connections between what they already know and what they are learning, when they can relate it to their experiences and get more meaning out of them, when they can see how ideas relate to each other, and when they can use what he has learned in concrete cases (Brown, 1994; Gardner, 1991; Shulman, 1987; Darling-Hammond, 1993).

Then, if both teacher training institutions and the schools where they work focus more on the learning process than teaching, this would put the subject learning in the foreground. Operating an intentional training organization to offer diversified learning experiences, identifying and enhancing different learning styles, generating environments and spaces to learn in circles with oneself or other colleagues, growth results in a dialectical spiral individually or collectively.

It is imperative to think of schools as learning spaces for teachers, students and parents, from a horizontal, participatory, reflection, debate, and collaboration model, based on the research of the teaching practice itself.

This shift in educational priorities requires working from self-management, autonomy and self-learning at school. Building combined routes from different aspects of professional development can include documentation of pedagogical experiences, refresher courses and workshops, exchange of successful pedagogical experiences, mutual professional support among colleagues, reading, discussion of bibliography, case analysis workshops, lectures and panels in charge of experts, among others. It is necessary to greatly increase the intellectual stimuli and opportunities that provide the true development of understanding and competence (Cohen, McLaughlin, & Talbert, 1993; Gardner, 1991).

The focus on learning, however, cannot be limited only to the spaces of the classroom because in order to truly generate circles of learning and spiraling teacher growth, it is necessary to expand the spaces from where teachers dialogue, interact, build, learn, unlearn, meet, and find each other.

And although the teacher's room, the hallways of the school, visits to bookstores, libraries, museums or cafeterias are considered non-formal or informal learning spaces, it is in these places where previous ideas are discussed before putting into practice, opinions of colleagues are calibrated, and sketches of ideas are made that suggest and connect everyday life in the classroom with a flexible use of disciplinary knowledge.

Hence the importance of looking at teaching from its visible and invisible spaces, and unraveling its true essence as an activity that develops in a set of intense and systematic relationships in a complex society (Imbernón, 2017). It is undeniable that the meaning, implications, spaces and scope of teaching and learning have been transformed and have exceeded the limits of the classroom.

Making visible the non-formal and informal learning of teachers

The traditional ways of teaching and learning are no longer functional because society and students have transformed. Spaces have been expanded to include learning, access to information, and the exchanging of ideas and communication. Nevertheless, educational objectives, teaching methods, and teaching environments, remain practically unalterable. (Vaillant, 2005). It is of great relevance, especially if we think the countries that have experienced greater educational success are those that have systematically fostered flexibility and innovation in teaching and learning (Hargreaves, 2008).

But then, how is learning placed in teacher training? How are all types and scenarios of teacher learning in formal contexts made visible and given value? What are the implications and meanings of teacher training? Do they embrace invisible learning?

The technical-professional world requires knowledge, skills, and abilities that are not contemplated as part of teaching in the formal circuits of education. Considering this, Cobo & Moravec (2011) wonder: how are these critical skills gained? "And the results lead us to recognize that, even if they are not seen (nor measured, nor certified), we know that these learnings exist and that they are tremendously valuable for a talent economy" (Cobo & Moravec, 2011, p. 26).

Invisible learning, therefore, conceives an alternative to learning as a continuum that goes through different times and spaces. Invisible learning is viewed as a "search to remix ways of learning that include continuous doses of creativity, innovation, collaborative and distributed work, laboratories of experimentation as well as new forms of knowledge translation" (pp. 23-24).

Following Moravec, this learning demands a series of transformations and high flexibility, since it requires a change in tools, pedagogies and practices, to train nomadic students (who tomorrow will become adaptable experts). It also allows apprentices to act on their knowledge, applying what they have learned through the practical resolution of problems, including those that have not been previously resolved.

Only at the end of life, says Dilthey (op. cit., Nazaré, 2015), can the end of education be derived, with the individual life shaped by different scenarios and learning experiences. The teacher, for example, with basic cooking knowledge or who simultaneously works as a chef, understands that different people eat certain meals and cook them differently.

They also understand that there is not only one type of flavor, and thus a person can have lasting memories of specific experiences and meanings triggered by these flavors. But as people change, they change their tastes and preferences. Something that tasted good for someone ten years ago, may not be enjoyable today, due to a change of habits or health reasons.

Transferred to education, that same teacher can understand that their students differ from 10, 20, or 30 years ago; that their needs, references and contexts have changed. Even being students of the same school but of different shifts (morning, afternoon) affects learning. Each student also learns differently: for example, by using other tools to learn, they differ; their motivations to learn can be equally diverse. These differences require the teachers to provide an equal treatment of such differences at the time of teaching.

This transference teachers make by integrating learning from other informal or non-formal contexts mostly occurs unconsciously and unsystematically, without recognizing that this type of learning happened. They are neither empowered nor incorporated into formal contexts such as their teaching role in the school.

Another essential example that can result from remixing ways of learning, making it possible to learn from oneself and others, is when a teacher succeeds in the classroom. Students recognize the teacher's excellence, and their teaching practice is influential, not only with their students, but also with their colleagues. However, neither the teacher nor their colleagues identify with certainty what lies behind the impact of their teaching. So it is important to reflect on their performance and answer some questions, such as the ones mentioned below:

- Is your professional impact due to school learning or to another series of learning built in informal or non-formal spaces?
- How can one make this learning conscious?
- How can one contribute individual knowledge to collective knowledge with other colleagues?
- Are you aware of where or how these skills were developed?
- Is your professional impact due to learning in school or another series of learning that was built in informal or non-formal spaces?

Invisible learning allows the unconscious to become conscious, as individuals or groups change learning environments and expand their spectrum—including digital environments and Information and Communication Technologies - connecting and reproducing new knowledge, "without marrying any particular technology and without implying renouncing adaptation and continuous updating" (Cobo & Moravec, 2011, p. 35).

Invisible learning stimulates and enhances teachers' individual learning for their own benefits and for students or colleagues. It links them with other learning environments and helps them perceive and understand the clues about how a successful experience has been achieved. Unless they are not aware of them or do not become visible to them, they become ephemeral and do not repeat themselves.

Thus, the visibility of non-formal and informal learning allows us to take control of learning and becomes a non-reproducible experience, subject to critical-reflexive analysis and oriented towards change, improvement, and innovation. Innovative teaching practices can enable the visibility of informal and non-formal learning.

The obligatory question is: What kind of learning needs to be the focus of attention in the teacher's training process - visible or non-visible learning? The answer would be both. In the words of Fullan (2002), developing our capacities to learn and continue learning without giving way to the vicissitudes of change is one of the ways for the educational system to transform.

> *If more individuals act as apprentices and they connect themselves with their inner child's spirit and they speak to those who have different ideas than theirs, then it is likely that systems learn to change (pp. 10-11).*

It is therefore necessary to redirect initial and continuous teacher training, focusing on how and what teachers learn, without neglecting curricular and disciplinary contents. It is essential to build learning environments with a conscious understanding of teacher metacognition processes (what, why, for whom, and how to learn). Teachers thus need to become the designers of their own training through diversified educational spaces (linking formal, informal, non-formal learning, and serendipitous learning), adaptable (to new technologies), flexible (in time and space), and innovative (for exploring and generating new possibilities for learning).

Invisible learning, metacognition, and transfer processes

Returning to the question of how teachers learn, it is necessary to incorporate metacognition and distant transfer processes into the subject. The former allows one to predict their performance in varied tasks and to monitor their current levels of mastery and comprehension (Brown & Murphy, 1975; Flavell, 1973). The latter alludes to the ability of the subjects to solve a problem in a situation that differs greatly from the initial learning episode. Salomon & Perkins (1987), mention that a distant transfer (the transference of knowledge between seemingly unrelated concepts) is made less frequently and with greater difficulty than a near transfer (spontaneous and automatic transfer of highly practiced skills, with little need for reflective thinking) because the subject must perform an analysis and representation of the situation that allows one to determine what rules, principles and concepts learned one must apply.

Both processes, metacognition and distant transfer, allow the teacher to realize how they learn; what resources or cognitive-emotional tools they used; related fields of knowledge or contexts apparently distant from one another; and how one learning can apply to another, offering them a greater breadth of what is learned. It should be noted that "without an adequate level of knowledge no transfer can be expected, it is difficult if the subjects have learned in a single context, and is favored when learning in multiple contexts" (Bassok & Holyoak, 1989. op. cit., Gómez & Solaz-Portolé, 2012, p. 207).

It is possible to improve teachers' transfer process if we support them to control their metacognitive learning strategies, their resources and to assess the availability of their knowledge. (Gomez & Solaz-Portolé, 2012). Teachers in training or those who work professionally, must at all times know what they do, why they do it, how they learn and what they learn. Hence, not only is *learning to learn* necessary but also *learning to think* and *teaching to think*.

> **We must direct the authentic role of the school to help each person think and to teach to learn. The teacher has to teach (and learn) lifelong learning strategies. One of the current and future research priority areas is that of interventions in metacognitive strategies, their impact on the cognitive development of students and the transfer and durability of their effects on learning (Tesouro, 1992).**

It is unavoidable to develop the natural aptitude of human intelligence to locate all its information in a context and in a group. It is necessary to teach the methods that allow apprehending mutual relations and reciprocal influences between the parties and the whole in a complex world. Learning and teaching the principles of strategy allow facing the risks, the unexpected, the uncertain, and modify their development in virtue of the information gained along the way. According to Morín (1999), "it is necessary to learn to navigate in an ocean of uncertainties through archipelagos of certainties" (p. 11). To the increasingly wide and deep inadequacies between disunited, divided, compartmentalized knowledge and the realities or problems increasingly polydisciplinary, transversal, multidimensional, transnational, global, planetary, Morín views them as challenges for the education of the future.

Toward the construction of knowmad teacher profiles

It is necessary, therefore, to think about teacher training from an integral, systemic, non-fragmented vision, without separating formal and informal, non-formal, and serendipitous learning and scenarios, as proposed by Cobo & Moravec (2011).

Assessing invisible learning processes links scattered, defragmented knowledge with learning. "Learn what it means to be human, in such a way that everyone from where you are takes knowledge and awareness at the same time of your complex identity and your common identity to all other humans" (Morin, 1999, p. 10).

The development of invisible learning in the individual, initial training processes of future teachers is essential since organizational learning is not possible without prior personal development. Furthermore, professional spaces where teachers develop the empowerment of invisible learning along with advice and preparation among colleagues in collegiate academic bodies, are essential. Balancing the individual and the collective and the divergent and convergent between theory and practice to strengthen change and transformation, in spaces of creation, imagination and academic production should be sought.

Although education is a key element both for the development of human capital and for the futures of human development, it has paradoxically been conceived to change slowly (Cobo & Moravec, 2011, p. 66). In this context, introducing *knowmads* in spaces such as education, represent a real possibility to face common issues in teaching today with greater success, such as academic despair; intellectual isolation; lack of dialogue; self-critical reflection; the dismissal of the value of reading and writing; and the lack of trust between the same colleagues, and of the teachers towards the students.

Moravec (2013, p. 18) describes a *knowmad* as someone who is innovative, imaginative, creative, capable of working with practically anyone, anywhere, and at any time. Knowmads may reconfigure and contextualize their work space, whose learning and training environments go beyond the limits of the school spaces.

Now, by rethinking and reimagining the learning paths of the teachers themselves, the diversification of their spaces, resources and tools to learn and be open to relearn, in environments of change, innovation and educational transformation; the knowmad profile is a viable and relevant option to achieve all the above. In addition to other characteristics suggested for the teachers of the 21st century, the knowmad profile offers the possibilities so that these become permanent apprentices, that can respond to the complex and uncertain contemporary problems, and manage their own formation individually and collectively.

It is important to comment that the synthesized dimensions and characteristics of the teacher's profile of the 21st century that are proposed in Tables 1-4 at the end of this chapter are not mutually exclusive; they complement, touch, and interweave. I also sought to articulate the contributions of recognized authors that address training, learning, and teaching with documented experiences and analyzes with managers, teacher educators and students, derived from a research developed in the Normal School of Atizapán de Zaragoza, Mexico (Carreño, G, et al., 2018). In this investigation, in-depth interviews were conducted with managers, teachers and future teachers of a Normal School. Concurrently, academic debates with students, observations, free writing and memories of teaching practices were maintained. In summary, attempts were made to connect ideas, link theory with practice, join clues, and fill in some cracks in teacher training that were seen from theory and practice.

From this data, the need to build more flexible, adapted, and balanced teacher profiles for an authentic teacher was perceived. This includes the possibility of including in schools other types of scenarios and spaces where there is room for knowledge and learning. This is at first sight invisible and unlinked with each other, but form part of life itself and impact the integral learning of individuals.

Final reflections

In general, and based on what I present in this chapter, I have come to the following conclusions:

1. Reflecting on the ways of learning and teaching are key elements of "learning to learn" and "learning to teach." And as Alliaud (2011) mentions, before asking how to get teachers to teach better, it is necessary to ask yourself how to facilitate and ensure that teachers learn. Rather than asking how to get teachers to teach better, one must ask how to facilitate and ensure that teachers learn.

2. Teacher training and development must be seen from learning and those who learn before teaching and from the offer. It is not possible to continue asking teachers to perform in their classrooms what they do not see applied in their training (Torres, 1998).

3. Considering, also, that the knowledge and competences of teachers are the results not only of their professional training but also of lifelong learning, in and out of school, in the exercise of teaching and learning, and other invisible training activities. Training devices that, from authors such as Navarro and Verdisco (2000), should be based on autonomous, horizontal and collaborative learning; They are more effective in transforming their educational practices.

4. When there are teamwork and support in situ, in their classrooms, teachers can try new pedagogical-didactic strategies, contextualize them and analyze the difficulties that arise in real scenarios, as these they happen.

5. Teaching is undeniably a complex professional activity built with a kind of hybrid identity. It is a high and specialized disciplinary, theoretical, and methodological domain; but also incorporates elements related to the field of art, creation, intervention, the transformation of contexts and the construction of a unique, unrepeatable, and immeasurable subject. Like any work of art, passion, dedication, commitment, time, and subtle touches of innovation and imagination are required.

6. Conceiving teaching from this perspective implies a dissociation and balance between thought and action, between knowledge and doing, to guide us in the art of teaching. But it also implies conceiving the classroom as a workshop, a maker of teachers who experiment, rehearse, and make mistakes, but follow the path of the creation of transformation. Hence, students more than consumers, from this perspective, think as producers of knowledge and/or content. Also before teaching, learn to learn, learn to think, to weave links with others, to seek and find a sense of life and professional sense as teachers.

7. It is indisputably necessary to reclaim the practice of teaching as a privileged space for training and reflection: reflecting on what we do to learn is the key to the "reflective professional" (Schön, 1992).

End notes.

1. Profiles in Tables 6-9 developed by Carreño, M. G. & Méndez, A. M., based on the works of Cobo & Moravec (2011); Moravec (2013); Freire (1998); Alliaud (2017); Pardo Kuklinski (2018); & Schön (1992, 1998).

2. All translations of Spanish-language resources were done by the author.

Table 6. 21st century teacher profile: Knowmad.

Dimension	Characteristics
Deconstruction, unlearning, and reconstruction	Adaptable to different environments; Learns to unlearn; Imaginative, creative; Able to transform constantly; Innovative (assigns a new value to a process or product).
Lifelong and ubiquitous learning	Able to learn at any time, in any context, and with anyone; Promotes educational debate and inter-institutional exchange; Seeks the integration of knowledge and learning; Autonomously diversifies their forms, modalities, and learning scenarios.
Co-creation processes	Generates knowledge and learns to share it; Able to coordinate, link, and connect with others; Learning network designers and operators; Learns to trust others; Not afraid of failure or success.
Content and knowledge production	Able to think the unthinkable, the impossible, and the unconventional; Reads, generates, and shares written and oral productions; Produces didactic, multimedia, analog, and digital materials; Possesses digital skills and transmedia competences; Designs training environments enhanced by technology and innovation; Designs digital narratives of teaching and learning; Manages the digital citizenship of themselves and their school community; They do not live in or for technology—they work with it.

Table 7. 21st century teacher profile: Divergent.

Dimension	Characteristics
Manage uncertainty	Self-determined and able to solve complex, unknown, and unstructured problems; Able to design *chaordic* pedagogical structures (blends of chaos and order); Understand the complex, mutable, and unpredictable nature of education.
Teaching metacognition	Learn and teach to learn and think, looking for different cognitive-emotional routes; Operate their flexible, divergent, lateral, systematic, and adaptive thinking; Design thinking; Develop their higher-order learning transfer processes.
Transformers	Contributes value to people, organizations, networks, and institutions; Breaks routine, static and inert structures of academic and school life; Designers of individual and common learning spaces (courtyards, corridors, reading spaces, school gardens, etc.).
Thinking/acting strategically and proactively	Transcends school immediacy; Promotes education for sustainable development (ESD); Prepared to face the challenges of the present and the future; Dominates the methods and strategies of thought and prospective research; Promotes glocal citizenship.

Table 8. 21st century teacher profile: Craftsman.

Dimension	Characteristics
Recover the essence of primitive teaching and humanistic approach to training	Vocation and service ethics; Commitment, responsibility; Contagious passion for learning and teaching; Able to promote inclusion; Enthusiastic, sensitive, passionate, and humble; Know how to live from diversity and encounters with other cultures; Learn by doing, from self-direction, autonomy, and self-management.
Create sense (of life and professionalism)	Creators of cultures of trust; Exercises the social value of educating; Awareness of strengths, weaknesses, and opportunities; Able to connect and link people; Flexible sense of time in teaching and learning; Clear about why and for what we educate.
Generators of possibilities	Reveals the hidden potential of students; Fosters student skills such as *entreprenerds* (empowered academically and intellectually); Possesses negotiation skills, agreement, and conflict transformation; Exercises positive and transforming leadership; Develops their own basic and superior thinking skills and those of their students; Ability to create, recreate, and imagine; Enhances the paths and learning spaces of parents; Incorporates non-formal and incidental learning from parents to academic-cultural school projects.
Educational influencers (teaching and learning to be)	Forms and uniquely guides students; Manages their personal, emotional well-being and that of their school community; Positively influence the lives of their students; Inspires the entire school community to become better people, continue learning, transform and innovate contexts; Marginalizes inertia and lack of academic mobility and normalizes innovation and educational change.
Experience designers	Breaks curricular boundaries with a dose of creativity, experimentation, and innovation; Uses dialogical architectures for learning and teaching; Skills for remixing forms, disciplines, methodologies, and learning strategies; Able to link visible and invisible learning, formal, non-formal, incidental, serendipitous, and informal scenarios.

Table 9. 21st century teacher profile: Reflexive.

Dimension	Characteristics
For the practice	Uses systematic and intentional rationalization; Develops differentiation devices according to the context in which they operate; Interacts with theoretical knowledge; Disciplinary, pedagogical, and methodological domain.
Through the practice	Connects the curriculum with other knowledge inside and outside the school; Capable of making decisions in the face of unexpected situations that may result during the exercise of their profession; Learns to act and "knows how to do" from practice; Able to mobilize cognitive resources; Able to make appropriate, adapted, and relevant decisions; Assertive; Implements actions adapted to the situation; Adapts their methodologies to the new ways of learning of students.
Starting from practice	Strengthens their experiential learning, critically analyzing their action; Aware of their teaching and their metacognitive processes; Broadens their perspective of social contexts; Apply action-research resources; Autonomy and responsibility in action; Conceives the classroom as a place for experimentation and innovation; Able to experiment, investigate, and imagine; Overcomes theory-practice dichotomies; Organizes their own training continuously; Self-motivated and self-driven.

REFERENCES

Alliaud, A. (2017). *Los artesanos de la enseñanza. Acerca de la formación de maestros con oficio*. Buenos Aires: Paidós

Barrera, R. (2016). Sorprendizaje: Cómo acabar con una educación aburrida , *TEDxSevilla*. www.youtube.com/ watch?v=FXTQq7Ojp94

Bassok, M., & Holyoak, K. J. (1989). Interdomain transfer between isomorphic opics in algebra and physics. *Journal of Experimental Psychology: Learning, Memory, and Cognition*, *15*, 153-166.

Brown, L. (1994). The advancement of learning, *Educational Researcher*, *23*(8), 4-12.

Brown, A.L., & Murphy, M.D. (1975). Reconstruction of arbitrary versus logical sequences by preschool children. *Journal of Experimental Child Psychology*, *20*(2), 307-326.

Carroll, L. (2000). *Alice's adventures in Wonderland*. A Chicago: BookVirtual Digital Edition. www.adobe.com/be_ en/active-use/pdf/Alice_in_ Wonderland.pdf

Carreño, M.G., Méndez A.M., Toledano, S.L., & Chávez, A.G.I. (2018). Reimaginando la formación y desarrollo docente desde la perspectiva de sus protagonistas. Proceedings from *Academia Journals Celaya, Guanajuato, Mexico, noviembre 7, 8, and 9, 2018*.

Cobo, C., & Moravec, J.W. (2011). *Aprendizaje Invisible: Hacia una nueva ecología de la educación*. Barcelona: Laboratori de Mitjans Interactius / Publicacions i Edicions de la Universitat de Barcelona.

Cohen, D. K., McLaughlin, M. W., & Talbert, J.E. (Eds.) (1993). *Teaching for understanding: Challenges for policy and practice*. San Francisco: Jossey-Bass.

Darling-Hammond, L. (1993). *Reframing the school reform agenda: Developing the capacity for school transformation*. Arlington, VA: Phi Delta Kappan.

Darling-Hammond, L. (2005). *El derecho aprender Crear buenas escuelas para todos*. Barcelona: Ariel Educación.

Esteve, J.M. (1994). *El malestar docente*. Barcelona: Paidós.

Esteve, J.M. (2003). *La tercera revolución educativa: La educación en la sociedad del conocimiento*. Barcelona: Paidós.

Esteve, J.M. (2006). Las emociones en el ejercicio práctico de la docencia. *Teoría de la Educación, 18*, 85-107.

Fernández, E.M. (1995). *La escuela a examen: Un análisis sociológico para educadores otras personas interesadas.* Madrid: Pirámide.

Flavell, J.H. (1973). Metacognitive aspects of problem-solving. In L. B. Resnick (Ed.), *The nature of intelligence.* Mahwah, NJ: Lawrence Erlbaum Associates..

Freire, P. (1997). *Pedagogía de la autonomía.* Buenos Aires: Siglo XXI.

Freire, P. (1998) *Teachers as cultural workers: Letters to those who dare teach.* Boulder, CO: Westview Press.

Fullan, M. (2002). *Las fuerzas del cambio: Explorando las profundidades de la reforma educativa.* Madrid: Akal Ediciones.

Galeano, E. (2005) *Legs up: The school of the world upside down.* Madrid: Edition square.

Gardner, H. (1991). *The unschooled mind: How children think and how schools should teach.* New York: Basic Books.

Gómez, B.C., & Solaz-Portolés, J.J. (2012). *Una revisión de los procesos de transferencia para el aprendizaje y enseñanza de las ciencias.* Valencia: Universitat de València.

Gonzalez, J.M. (2009). *The evaluation based on research as a theory of metacompleja learning and teaching.* La Paz: III CAB.

Hargreaves, A. (2008). Leading professional learning communities. In A. Blankstein, P. Houston, & R. Cole (Eds.), *Sustaining professional learning communities.* Thousand Oaks, CA: Corwin Press.

Imbernón, F. (2017). *Ser docente en una sociedad compleja: La difícil tarea de enseñar.* Barcelona: Editorial Graó.

Lombardi, G. (1998). Formación docente en instituciones de formación. In a cooperative seminar for the transformation of teacher training, Mar del Plata, Argentina.

Nazaré, M., & Amaral, P. (2015) Dilthey y la educación. *Revista Educación y Pedagogía [S.l.], 26-27*(Sept. 2015), 107-121. aprendeenlinea.udea.edu.co/revistas/index.php/revistaeyp/article/view/24380

Moravec, J.W. (Ed.). (2013). *Knowmad Society.* Minneapolis: Education Futures.

Morin, E. (1990). *Introducción al pensamiento complejo.* Spain: Editorial Gedisa.

Morin, E. (1999). *La cabeza bien puesta: Repensar la reforma, reformar el pensamiento.* Argentina: Nueva vision editores.

Navarro, J.C., & Verdisco A. (2000). *Teacher training in Latin America: Innovations and trends.* (No.EDU-114). Washington, DC: Inter-American Development Bank.

Nóvoa, A. (2009). Para una formación de profesores construida dentro de la profesión. *Revista de Educación (Ministerio de Educación, España), 359,* 203-218.

Pardo, H.K. (2018). *El maestro debe ser un diseñador de experiencias de aprendizaje.* Interview for INEVERY CREA. ineverycrea.mx/comunidad/ineverycreamexico/recurso/entrevista-del-mes-a-hugo-%20pardo-kuklinski-el/a9ca040d-2735-7a3b-ea60-0fb8864ba9c4

Perrenoud, P. (2004). *Desarrollar la práctica reflexive en el oficio de enseñar: Profesionalización y razón pedagógica.* Barelona, Graó.

Richert, A.E. (2005). Inquiring about practice: Using web-based materials to develop teacher inquiry. *Teaching Education, 16*(4), 297-310.

Schön, D.A. (1992). *La formación de profesionales reflexivos. Hacia un nuevo diseño de la enseñanza y el aprendizaje en las profesiones.* Barcelona: Paidós.

Schön, D.A. (1998). *El profesional reflexivo: Cómo piensan los profesionales cuando actúan.* Barcelona: Paidós.

Shulman, L. (1987) Knowledge andteaching: Foundations of the new reform. *Harvard Educational Review, 57*(1).

Salomon, G., & Perkins, D.N. (1987). Transfer of cognitive skills from programming: When and how? *Journal of Educational Computing Research, 3*(2), 149.

Tedesco, J.C., & Tenti, F.E. (2002). Nuevos tiempos y nuevos maestros. Proceedings from *Regional Conference on Teachers Performance in Latin America and the Caribbean: New Priorities, Brasilia, 2002.* unesdoc.unesco. org/ark:/48223/pf0000134675

Tesouro, M. (1992). *Optimization of intellectual performance from computerized programming.* Barcelona: Autonomous University of Barcelona.

Torres del Castillo, R.M. (1998). Nueva función docente Qué modelo de formación y para qué modelo educativo? *Perfiles Educativos, 82*(octubre-diciembre).

Vaillant, D. (2005). *Formación docente en América Latina: Reinventar el modelo tradicional.* Barcelona: Octaedro.

Gabriela Carreño Murillo is a knowmad, *civilizionaria*, teacher educator, designer of learning experiences, and a teaching craftsman. She graduated from the Normal School of Atizapán de Zaragoza, Mexico and completed postgraduate studies at the Complutense University of Madrid, Spain. She works at the Normal School of Atizapán de Zaragoza, developing the research around training and invisible learning, and is affiliated with the Ceibal Foundation (Uruguay). cesoe2014@gmail.com

Notes

Notes

Notes

REI School: A school to fit any child

ERIK MILETIĆ

Introduction

Schools in most countries are designed as institutions that enable children to use their talents and skills to contribute to our societies. However, the modern schooling system seems to have an impact on the general happiness of attendees due to an overreliance on verbal and numerical intelligence, thus primarily developing skills for information retention. This may suggest that the only difference between the mind of a child and that of an adult is in the quantity of information that they retain. In addition, children are objectified and their individual abilities and intelligence are not being considered. Passive learning by listening and acquiring abstract concepts is enforced, although I believe children's brains frequently do not have a capacity for this.

The above may be the cause for most difficulties that are currently seen in school children: lack of interest in school, reading difficulties and more evident depression and even suicide because of failing in school. The fact that children learn best through associations that are developed in practical application is completely ignored. These associations are based on pictures and feelings for as long as they are accompanied by pleasure, fun, challenge, and safety. These may be achieved easily by experiencing (playing), but not through notes, definitions, and theories in strictly managed time intervals.

If things are to change, we need to encourage creativity in children by planning for a future education system that relies on experience and fun, but also on respect for different ways of thinking in children and adults, taking into account individual differences regarding interests and skills among children.

I believe the REI model ("Eros," 2012; Kenda 2014) offers a novel understanding of the human psyche and is based on the following assumptions:

- Our minds are made up of a combined activity of three autonomous intellectual systems: *Reason*, *Emotion*, and *Instinct*. While each intellect 'thinks' in a specific way, only *Reason* generates our conscious thoughts. And so, we experience decisions made through Emotion and Instinct as our subconscious.
- In the process of growing up, the three intellectual systems develop and establish a hierarchy in their inter-relationships that persists throughout the lifetime. It is this hierarchy that determines our aptitude for certain skills and our lack of interest for others.

Emotion and *Instinct* learn through experience and play because they memorise associations. Only Reason is capable of abstract learning through books and lectures. The principal problem in education today is that it mostly caters to areas that fall within Reason, including language, mathematics, and logic. A more advanced and inclusive school system would provide a choice of subjects that correspond to the dominant intellectual system of an individual while allowing him/her to gain only basics in other areas. The grades would be based on exams in subjects that correspond to the dominant intellectual system. This chapter offers a detailed explanation of the REI model in relation to the recent discoveries in psychology, pedagogy and neuroscience and demonstrates their application in building of better education and society.

My vision of the best educational institution for young children is a place that children would go to feeling happy, primarily because this kind of school would enable realization of their individual potential. They would achieve this through pursuit of their own interests and through the encouragement of self-expression, thus leading to the discovery of personal talents. This approach would lead to growth and gathering of individual skills that children will use when they mature, which would benefit society in a multitude of ways.

Children cannot and do not think in the same way as adults. However, adults write school textbooks, teach and determine what is acceptable, and determine what is not in a child's world. My sense is that children learn best through experience and by associating images, motions, and feelings with particular ideas. Instead, the standard way in which adults teach children to assimilate new information is often through study of theory and abstractions, delivered in a linear and logical way, which is most frequently inaccessible to a young child's understanding. Despite these realizations, we continue to teach children as if they are adults, using suboptimal textbooks and poorly mapped-out educational approaches. The end result is frequently demeaning, problems are multiple while adult mind that created the issues is mostly unable to comprehend the causes, let alone find the solutions. The REI model offers new insights into how our minds work and can be of assistance in this situation.

Introducing the REI model

The REI model was created by Igor Kenda's *[psi]* book (2012) and is based on a core assumption that our mind comprises three independent intellectual modules which become organized in a hierarchical relationship as we grow up. The hierarchy of these intellectual modules generates the way we think. The REI model is very simple, but yet complex, and I believe it can help build perspectives into many phenomena of the human psyche such as falling in love, happiness, and love—and difficulties such as dyslexia, ADHD/ADD, depression, addiction, and phobias. The universal application of the REI model is evident in its use in forming social structures and their changes. As the intellectual modules have presumed locations in our brains, I argue that the model can potentially also be used in neurology and neuroscience.

This chapter offers an introduction into the REI model to the extent that is necessary for its application in education. It also provides practical guidance and ideas for a school that will be a good fit for every child. Let us start with a short presentation of the REI model, followed by a more detailed description of its basic settings.

Short description of the REI model

Based on REI model, our mind is thought to comprise a combined activity and cooperation of three autonomous intellectual systems termed Reason, Emotion and Instinct (together, "REI"). Each intellect is unique and distinct from the other two, using its own different perception of the world, harnessing its own desires, motives, will, goals, memories, interests, understanding of who we are and the world round us, and the power of decision-making. All intellects are self-aware. However, only Reason thinks conscious thoughts. Emotion thinks in images and governs movement while Instinct deals with emotions that are linked to feelings of safety and/or danger.

While we are growing up, I argue that the three intellects compete with one another to create the final hierarchy in their relationship. This hierarchy subsequently remains unchanged in the mind of a healthy individual for the rest of their life. The hierarchy that is finally reached at adulthood (around the age of 25) not only persists, but is deemed to define our character.

On the foundations of our REI character, our psyche consists of our world and our house. 'Our world' is our unique understanding of the world around us and the people we meet in it, while 'our house' is our unique understanding of us within that world. Each intellectual module can be anywhere on the spectrum between accepting and rejecting its house and/or its world. The result of acceptance of all three intellectual modules determines the level at which we, as persons, accept our world and/or our house.

In the state of self-acceptance, an intellectual module (or intellect) will seek the truth knowing that it can only see some of it. It will want to cooperate with other modules within oneself or with other people. Every failure is interpreted as part of that journey towards truth and is talked about with the same ease as a success. Being self-accepted means that each intellectual module will not see itself as being more or less worthy than others, irrespective of what qualities of faults it may have. We only perceive its own opinions and those of others as information that is shared and not solicited.

Conversely, in the state of self-rejection, an intellectual module believes it is faulty and can therefore not be loved, respected, happy, and accepted in society the way it really is (with all of its faults and qualities, failures and successes), so it uses its skills to conceal the faults or to embellish them to gain reputation, respect and social acceptance. These mechanisms of concealment are termed 'stage decorations.' A person in the state of rejection identifies with his/her stage decorations, believing that such pretence will lead to happiness, respect, and love and will therefore interpret everything that points towards those false stage decorations as a direct attack on self.

In the state of rejection, the intellect becomes selfish and will cooperate only with those who validate their stage decorations. The stage decorations can be almost anything, ranging from make-up, accumulation of valuables, business or academic careers, and any other pretence. Persons who are in a state of rejection can be very successful in the field of their dominant intellect (that rejects itself), driven by the fear that someone might look behind the stage decorations and discover the truth. However, they can never attain inner happiness because happiness is a product of satisfaction of all three intellectual modules. It is possible that a person in the state of rejection may accept her or his own faults and stop concealing those by stage decorations. For as long as she or he believes to be less worthy than others, the person remains in a state of rejection. Self-rejection of the intellect is usually a result of the environment (e.g., parents, society, or school) not enabling an individual to develop his/her skills or not respecting its values when one learns from their teachers that he/she is more or less valued than others.

The REI model stipulates that the feeling of inner happiness is a consequence of all three intellects being contented, which happens when we live our lives in a way that enables the values and the skills of all the three intellects to be fulfilled. This kind of happiness is not dependent on achievements and external validation; therefore, anyone can be happy.

The intellects not only function on a personal level but also on the level of any society, any state or even globally. It is part of the evolution of the intellects and it is observed by having people who share the way they see the world joining into groups, which usually means they share the same dominant intellect(s). The more political power a group has, the more influence it will have on the social structure, laws, norms, and education. In this scenario, the values of one intellect are dominant to the detriment of the two other intellects. This results in ever more difficult acceptance of the intellects which possess values that are neither represented nor respected, leading to their increased dissatisfaction. When the level of dissatisfaction among people with dominant intellects that are being undermined by the society reaches a critical mass, they start collaborating and forming a two-third majority that is typically sufficient for a revolution whereby the only thing sought is a change of the intellect in power. Each intellect develops the social structure that responds to its values. Reason creates capitalism or finally the corporate world that puts the interest of a legal entity above that of a physical entity (human being). Emotion creates a feudal/slavery society and Instinct forms a socialist society or a dictatorship. Modern education is structured on values of Reason and neglects the skills of Emotion and Instinct. However, I posit that the only education in a just society is the one that equally respects the values of all three intellects. This is because of the influence of Reason that any school reform will remain within its boundaries and will have no positive effects.

Intellects change throughout our lives but they do not mature with the same speed or intensity as they are linked to their function in our bodies. I believe that Reason will continue to develop its functions until the age of 25, while Emotion and Instinct will most likely mature in puberty. This means it is very important in education to put more emphasis on the development of skills governed by Emotion and Instinct and to combine them progressively with those of Reason.

Key guidelines for a school that will fit any child

Based on the short outline above, we can conclude that the solution that the REI model suggests is a school system that:

- Respects and develops values, skills, and intelligence of all the three intellects equally as they mature; and,
- Respects individual differences that result from a hierarchy of character, meaning that we should not force the skills of all the three intellects onto individuals, but individuals should be able to choose what they are interested in, while doing the required minimum in other areas.

I believe it is necessary to transfer these experiences onto society so that the values and the skills of all three intellects can be equally represented and respected.

The REI model is somewhat related to the educational experiences from Finland

The Finnish education system has achieved a model of governance that is closest to the ideas held by the REI model. Different types of intelligence and skills that originate from particular intellects are equally represented, and it strongly encourages cooperation between the intellects. Any school system that promotes development of only one intellect is very damaging because individuals need all the three intellects for optimal functioning.

I would like to stress that it is not necessary to force each child to develop all the different intellects, but to give them freedom of choice instead. If their choices please their dominant intellect, it will become more prone to give in to subordinate intellects, especially if it realises the advantage it may have from cooperation. The more acceptance there are among the three intellects, the more willing they become to cooperation and stepping aside when that proves to be the better solution for the individual in question.

Three autonomous intellects as the sum of our consciousness and unconsciousness

Each intellect opposes the characteristics of the other two intellects. Since Reason is the only intellect that has conscious thoughts, we have, for the lack of better understanding, ascribed the activities of Emotion and Instinct to the unconscious and have been filing all the things we could not understand into that same cabinet. However, the REI model offers a much better understanding because it claims that Emotion and Instinct can also have leading roles in 'thinking' and decision-making. Since these two intellects mature much quicker than Reason, it would be wise to depend on and utilise them when planning the future of education. The REI model offers a detailed description of how Emotion and Instinct think, what goals they have, and how they learn and memorise. Let us start considering Reason first, as it is the only one that we are readily aware of and one we most frequently identify with.

Reason

As far as Reason is concerned, we can say that it thinks verbally and is responsible for all of our conscious thoughts and activities as well as for our conscious perceptions. Its thoughts and thinking are created by the regular sequencing of words from letters and numbers and by making concepts, sentences, definitions, and theories. It is focused on details, verifiable, and perceivable; in other words, it is material and repeatable. It thinks linearly and can therefore connect causes and consequences, demonstrating a logical way of thinking which is its main mode of operating. Because of its capacity for linear thinking, it can put past events into a sequence while also being capable of step-by-step long-term planning.

Reason forms opinions by observing material evidence, analysis and risk management using logic, and statistics and probability. It likes to use procedures and instructions that require a step-by-step approach and are executed in a precise order. It is focused on details, likes structure, rules, laws, and time schedules. It enjoys holding academic titles, diplomas, and licenses.

Reason also interprets for us what Emotion and Instinct are thinking and this process is experienced by us as being conscious of our feelings: desires, attraction, pleasure, happiness, and phobias. All the same, feelings are created by Emotion and Instinct, while Reason functions by naming, categorising, and giving feelings appropriate verbal connotation- thoughts.

Reason is motivated by a need for the ownership of material goods, theoretical knowledge, and any evidence of having gained theoretical knowledge. In the state of rejection, the ownership of goods and knowledge is not geared towards personal growth, the search of truth, or the betterment of society, but solely as a camouflage of 'shortcomings,' namely feelings of low self-worth and self-grandeur in society. Its academic knowledge and material possessions become mere stage decorations. In the state of rejection, Reason becomes greedy, stingy, and does not understand any other values unless it sees self-interest. As it refuses to include the other two intellects in thinking, it becomes heartless and cannot see the bigger picture while any practical experience it may have is of no value unless it is 'validated' by academic authority and confirmation of self-beliefs.

An optimal school for Reason

We can see that modern education is based predominantly on Reason as it values mathematics, language, and logical thinking the most with reliance on material evidence and IQ tests. Learning is mostly verbal and theoretical, scheduled in exact time slots that give no space for feelings, pleasure, fun, or game. And, it provides no space for learning by experience, movement, or solving practical problems that require innovation or creativity. We expect teamwork from adults and yet we isolate children by seating them at desks in accordance to their respective age groups. Children have no idea what they are learning, why they are learning these things, or how they connect with real life.

This kind of education is pushing most children, especially those with dominant Emotion or Instinct intellect, into a state of deep rejection and a person who does not accept himself is easier to manipulate because he or she is only thinking with its dominant intellect. This kind of education is boring to the intellect of Emotion because it does not encourage its skills or practical application, and Reason labels this as a 'learning difficulty.' Because of a lack of opportunities to validate itself, I believe it often resorts to violence and addiction. Instinct can also not find self-realisation in this form of education and it feels rejected and finds shelter in withdrawal into the inner world where it feels safe.

I also believe this kind of education creates inner conflicts between intellects which results in depression. Unfortunately, modern education has become a filter that only children with a dominant Reason can pass, and they will end up receiving degrees and licences that will enable them to play leading roles in society, to make and pass laws, and setting social norms–including those relating to education.

If you think that is not the right way to go, let's get to know Emotion and Instinct, find out how they think, learn, and memorise, and what schools would they like to have. Once we acquaint ourselves with them, we will have a solid foundation to build a school fit for every child.

Emotion

Emotion is an intellect that thinks spontaneously in images, movement, and colours. It controls our motor skills, spatial perception, and our sexual drive. It is the intellect that creates feelings in our brains, such as pleasure, curiosity, but also rage and anger if the images it desires do not take place here and now.

Because of the way it thinks and the functions it has in our bodies, Emotion is prone to developing its abilities in the areas of motor skills and image expression, hence it usually manifests as an excellent sportsman, dancer, or a musician; but can also be an architect, a painter, a poet—an artist, a comedian, an imitator, an actor, and a director. It is very good at improvising, motivating, and innovating. It is very sociable and extroverted, can be an excellent team worker, and as it knows no fear. It is a born leader, a soldier, a martial arts champion, a firefighter, a pilot, or an astronaut. If it cooperates well with Reason, it can be an excellent programmer or mathematician but also an entrepreneur or a manager.

It is motivated by a competitive spirit and a constant drive for improvement, simplification, and problem solving. If it is in a state of acceptance, those who are better will be an example to follow and will serve as motivation for self-improvement. It learns by doing or by observing. I can say it that the more practice Emotion has the better its thinking becomes.

Emotion communicates verbally by trying to convert images into words. In this situation, Reason and Emotion may fight each other and the result is a stutter. However, Emotion mostly communicates non-verbally, through the way it looks at you using its body language and movement, intonation, onomatopoeia, and touch—and some kind of "telepathy" when it becomes "one" with its surroundings or when it connects "telepathically" with its partner, a friend, or members of the group or team in which it belongs.

If a school does not stimulate the development of Emotion's skills and values, the intellect can fall into a state of rejection and start using its skills to prove its value. Its competitive spirit becomes overbearing, and it strives to be the best at any cost and will even be prepared to eliminate competitors. It becomes prone to violence or tries to validate itself through sexuality. When facing problems that it cannot solve, it deteriorates into addictive behaviour. In schools, and in educational formats that do not allow children to develop motor skills and visualisation, they retreat to video games as a safe escape into a world that does not put constraints on them and does not judge them and yet allows them to develop those skills.

Theoretical learning and sitting at school desks is boring for Emotion because it is not challenging and because it does not see any practical application especially if there are no hands on learning involved. When faced with a task that holds no interest, Emotion loses concentration and can therefore become labelled by Reason as having learning difficulties. It is much easier to diagnose someone with ADHD or ADD than to admit one's own difficulty, lack of understanding or even inability to create an education that would challenge and develop Emotion.

As Reason has become the dominant intellect in our society, our world has become more and more switched off to the values of Emotion, except for situations in which Reason enjoys material benefits from them (e.g., profit from sports or arts). As this intellect is more often dominant in men, it is among them that we usually find the mentioned interests, skills, and difficulties.

An optimal school for Emotion

A school that would make Emotion happy and able to achieve self-realisation must be based on the development of motor and/or visual skills through play for younger children and practical problem solving for older youth. Learning should continue for as long as it is interesting, challenging enough, and should involve experts showcasing their skills, thus serving as inspiration. A competitive spirit ought to be fostered to promote self-learning with victory as an achievement of personal bests.

Instinct

Evolutionally Instinct is the oldest of the three intellects and is therefore in charge of controlling our most vital functions, inner organs, immune system, epigenetic and genetic regulation, and is in direct control of feelings such as warmth, weight, pain, smell, and taste. It thinks through feelings that it links to danger or safety. Reason recognises its signal for danger as the feeling of fear.

It is also the intellect that our imagination originates from which is primarily used by Instinct to anticipate danger and protect our health, but also to look for new possibilities to change the environment. By nature, Instinct is introverted, suspicious, very careful, attentive, caring, and altruistic. When cooperating with Reason, it can be an excellent inspector able to "detect" a problem, but also as a journalist because of its capacity for criticism.

Instinct can be excellent in the medical profession, in veterinary science, and in natural healing that relies on stimulation of immune system. It works with taste and smell testing and work with plants, but also in education, abnormal psychology, and in the most difficult job on the planet: motherhood. That is when its ability to do something because it needs to be done is best served and it does so not expecting much in return, except a bit of attention. Instinct has a strong need for social equality, human rights, and animal rights.

As Instinct is very creative, it has an excellent sense of humour, but because it is introverted, it does this in the background instead. It prefers to write screenplays rather than taking centre stage of a performance. Because it is afraid of not being accepted, it will often refrain from contributing ideas and may pass them onto someone else. When cooperating with Emotion, it becomes brave and this combination can produce excellent creative results, such as in styling and fashion.

Instinct communicates verbally by trying to convert its feelings of fear or safety into words, but like Emotion, it mostly communicates non-verbally through body language or through senses (e.g., smells) that are not accessible by Reason. It is likely that Instinct also possesses seemingly 'telepathic' skills that stem from the subconscious, such as occasions when it is trying to warn us of danger. We perceive this as our intuition.

Instinct is motivated by envy, its need to possess what makes other people happy. Because of it is overly cautious, it would rather imitate someone than attempt something new on its own. When it is in a state of rejection, envy becomes very strong and turns into malice, as Instinct in that state does not believe it can be happy. It develops an unhealthy enjoyment of others' misfortune instead.

Emotion and Instinct do not speak in the language of Reason and therefore need to use their own 'language' to warn us of their dissatisfaction. In Instinct, that language is fear, which can turn into phobias, possessiveness, jealousy, need for total control, overwhelming feelings of guilt, and other emotional manipulation. It also controls our appetite and may manifest in various eating disorders such as bulimia and anorexia. I believe it also controls our fertility and immune system, and it can manipulate those into inappropriate states ranging from allergies to cancer. As this intellect is more frequently dominant in women, the aforementioned interests, skills, and difficulties are more often found in women. Because Instinct also learns by doing or through empathy, it does not find the school of Reason to its benefit.

An optimal school for Instinct

Instinct develops by adjusting and cooperating with nature with care for all the living creatures at the core of its thinking. School subjects such as environmental science or biology that are taught through the use of books written by Reason have nothing in common with the way Instinct perceives nature and the creatures within it. Like Emotion, it also learns by doing. It needs to work in nature, to care for it, to care for clean water and natural food, and to look after its own immune system as the key factor of our good health and in contrast to use of medication as preferred by Reason. It needs to care for animals and those in need of help. It enjoys gardening and organic food cultivation and preparation. It looks for herbs and tea plants and makes tea and medicinal potions. It arranges flowers and uses hands for any kind of creative expression such as writing. All the above would cater to development of empathy, care for others and social equality, creativity and the love for nature and harmony with all living creatures.

REI School: a school to fit any child

The foundation of a REI school comprises equal inclusion of all the three intellects in the process of learning and memorising as well as equal development of their skills and respect for their values.

A REI school would combine three basic groups of subjects under the three intellects, with teaching of those subjects founded on their different ways of thinking, learning, and memorising. Each group of subjects would also have two subgroups to capture different directions of the development of each intellect. These subgroups are:

- Reason: verbal and numerical subgroups;
- Emotion: motor and visual subgroups; and,
- Instinct: care and creative subgroups.

I argue the primary purpose of education is to develop students' ability and desire to think and learn about the world around them, thus enabling students to gain knowledge that covers various aspects of life, including cultural and developmental needs. In order for a learning process to be successful, pupils need to feel happy because in that state, they are more likely to engage in the process of learning fully. Happiness of all pupils could be achieved by providing children opportunities to choose more subjects from the group of their dominant intellect or by allowing them to learn those subjects at a much higher level in advanced classes or by attending classes with older students. An optimal school would begin as the school of Emotion or Instinct at a very early age and would include Reason as the years progress.

Another approach is to integrate children into real life as much as possible rather than isolating them in school buildings. That way, they would feel included and introduced to the wider public and could thus showcase their skills for the benefit of the community, applying what they have learned in school. This would enable them to use their innovative and creative skills, test theories, and make improvements. I believe such an approach would lead them onto the path of self-consciousness and would undoubtedly reduce the need for standing out by abusing alcohol and/or smoking.

Our mind functions best when all three intellects are cooperating. This cooperation fosters development of emotional and social intelligence that could be better indicators than the IQ testing of thinking processes that are dominated by Reason.

It is very important to respect individual differences in the process of learning. In other words, it is important to let children choose their education pathways. As much as we are sceptical of children knowing what is best for them, we only need to consider the validated experiences of free and democratic schools, some of which, like the Summerhill School in the United Kingdom, have a century-long tradition. Perhaps 100 years is a long enough time to show that a child does know when he or she is happy and that he or she naturally needs to learn or to get better at things—that is learning with ease.

An REI school would expect students to acquire a minimum base of knowledge of all the three intellects while they would use more advanced techniques in the fields that students are interested in and separation by age should not be used as a criterion for learning but their level of competence. I would expect teachers to be versed in the fields that correspond to their characters to be better placed to assist children in finding their own interests.

Evaluation of character under the REI model

Just as an 'average' person does not exist, an 'average grade' does not tell us anything about a student. Grading would better evaluate a student taking into consideration basic knowledge in the areas of the three intellects. The aim is to develop talent and not to stifle it by comparing it with someone who is average. I propose the following grading scheme in Table 10.

My proposed scheme shows a student's final grade (on a Likert-type scale of 1-5, whereby 5 conveys the highest value) relates only to an area or areas in which a student has the best development of a particular intellect. This promotes the development of talents and does not force a child to grow in an area

Table 10. Evaluation matrix for a REI school.

Student	Reason		Emotion		Instinct		Final character/grade
	Numerical	Verbal	Motor	Visual	Care	Creativity	
S1	5	3	2	4	4	2	5 numerical: Reason / R
S2	2	2	5	2	4	2	5 motor: Emotion / Ei
S3	3	3	3	2	4	3	4 care: Instinct / I
S4	2	5	3	5	3	3	5 verbal: Reason & 5 visual: Emotion / RE
S5	2	3	4	4	5	5	5 care & 5 creativity: Instinct / I

that he/she is not good at. Although grades are seldom an objective reflection of a pupil, they may serve as an approximate measure of the current state, thus providing motivation for personal development going forward.

Conclusion

I believe the REI model offers an excellent foundation and guidelines for a school that would fit any child while respecting all the three intellects and the resulting individual's character. This is presented as a first step and provides a lot of room to acquaint yourself with the three intellects and to use this knowledge in your profession, creatively and innovatively, and in cooperation with children. REI schools would therefore help kids identify their strengths by exploring their talents from a very young age and growing their skills over their years in school.

However, all the effort we may put in will not work if change is limited to school and education because it also has to involve our society. This may take time and will be driven by a realisation that the current operating systems in many societies are no longer fit for the purpose they were built. At what precise point this need for change will arise is likely to vary by society, its moral values, and its level of social awareness. Therefore, this is a rather complex issue that I believe will happen in waves across the globe as societies develop.

REFERENCES

"Eros". (2012). *[psi]*. Maribor, Slovenia: DCC Marketing.

Kenda, I. (2014). REI method for elimination of dyslexia. *Journal of Psychology and Psychotherapy Research, 1,* 69-85.

Erik Miletic graduated from the Ljubljana University Faculty of Computer and Information Science in Slovenia and has a professional background in information technology. Since 2010, he has studied the REI model and its application in various fields.
erik.miletic@gmail.com

Notes

Notes

Notes

Appendix
Manifesto 15: Evolving learning

January 1, 2015

Many of the most inspiring documents are strongly associated with a date. The U.S. Declaration of Independence was signed on July 4, 1776; Charter 77 emerged in January 1977; Dogme 95 was crafted in 1995. Ideas transform and develop over time. This manifesto represents a snapshot of our ideas, visions for the future, and what we have learned to date about learning and education. This text serves as a reference point to help us understand how we've done so far and what actions we need to take next.

In a world consumed with uncertainty and a growing sense of the obsolescence of our education systems, how can we ensure the success of ourselves as individuals, our communities, and the planet? We need to evolve education.

What we have learned so far

1. **"The future is already here – it's just not very evenly distributed"** (William Gibson in Gladstone, 1999). The field of education lags considerably behind most other industries largely from our tendency to look backward, but not forward. We teach the history of literature, for example, but not the future of writing. We teach historically important mathematical concepts, but do not engage in creating new maths needed to build the future. Moreover, everything "revolutionary" taking place in learning has already happened at different scales, in bits and pieces, at different places. The full impacts for ourselves and our organizations will be realized when we develop the courage to learn from each other's experiences and accept the risk and responsibility in applying a futures orientation in our praxis.

2. **1.0 schools cannot teach 3.0 kids.** We need to redefine and build a clear understanding of *what* we are educating for, *why* we do it, and *for whom* our educational systems serve. Mainstream compulsory schooling is based on an outdated, 18th century model for creating citizens with the potential to become loyal, productive factory workers and bureaucrats. In the post-industrial era, this should no longer be the end goal of education. We need to support learners to become innovators, capable of leveraging their own imagination and creativity to realize new outcomes for society. We do this because today's challenges cannot be solved through old thinking. And, we are all co-responsible for creating futures with positive outcomes that benefit all people in the world.

3. **Kids are people, too.** All students must be treated and respected as human beings with recognized, universal human rights and responsibilities. This means students must have an active say in the choices regarding their learning, including how their schools are run, how and when they learn, and all other areas of everyday life. This is inclusion in a real sense. Students of all ages must be afforded liberties to pursue educational opportunities and approaches for learning that are appropriate for them, as long as their decisions do not infringe on the liberties of others to do the same (adapted from EUDEC, 2005).

4. **The thrill of jumping off a cliff by deciding to do so yourself is a high you will never have if someone else pushes you off of it.** In other words, the top-down, teacher-student model of learning does not maximize learning as it devours curiosity and eliminates intrinsic motivation. We need to embrace flat, horizontalized, and distributed approaches to learning, including peer learning and peer teaching, and empower students to realize the authentic practice of these modes. Educators must create space to allow students to determine if, and when, to jump off the cliff. Failing is

a natural part of learning where we can always try again. In a flat learning environment, the teacher's role is to help make sure the learner makes a well-balanced decision. Failing is okay, but the creation of failures is not.

5. **Don't value what we measure, measure what we value.** In our obsession with testing, we have somehow allowed the OECD to become the "world's ministry of education" through the PISA regime, and the cult of educational measurement is spreading throughout the world. At a national, state-to-state level, it is as if we are competing to be the best-looking kid in a humdrum family. Even worse, our schools are producing politicians and policy leaders that do not know how to interpret test scores. The best innovations are often killed the moment we start worrying about measurement. We need to put an end to compulsory testing and reinvest these resources into educational initiatives that create authentic value and opportunities for growth.

6. **If "technology" is the answer, what was the question?** We seem to obsess over new technologies while having little understanding of what they're for or how they can impact learning. Technologies are great for doing what we have been doing better, but using new technologies to do the same old stuff in the classroom is a lost opportunity. Black boards have been replaced by whiteboards and SMART Boards. Books have been replaced by iPads. This is like building a nuclear plant to power a horse cart. Yet, nothing has changed, and we still focus tremendous resources on these tools and squander our opportunities to exploit their potential to transform what we learn and how we do it. By recreating practices of the past with technologies, schools focus more on managing hardware and software rather than developing students' *mindware* and the *purposive* use of these tools.

7. **Digital skills are invisible, and so should technologies be in schools.** *Invisible learning* is a recognition that most of the learning we do is "invisible" – that is, it is through informal, non-formal, and serendipitous experiences rather than through formal instruction (Cobo & Moravec, 2011). It takes into account the impact of technological advances to enable the invisible spaces to emerge—but, like the spaces, the use of technologies is likewise invisible and fluid. If the challenge for our schools and governments is to create students that stand out in creativity and innovation, and not students that mindlessly memorize and repeat old ideas, any use of technologies for learning must enable these creative and innovative directions. Schools should not use computers to "do work" around preassigned parameters with prescribed outcomes; they should be used to help design and create products and learning outcomes that extend beyond the imagination of the curriculum. Rather than putting technology in the forefront and obscuring learning, make it invisible yet ambient, enabling learners to discover their own pathways for development with these tools.

8. **We cannot manage knowledge.** When we talk about knowledge and innovation, we frequently commingle or confuse the concepts with data and information instead. Too often, we fool ourselves into thinking that we give kids knowledge when we are just testing them for what information they can repeat. To be clear: *Data* are bits and pieces here and there, from which we combine into *information*. *Knowledge* is about taking information and creating meaning at a personal level. We *innovate* when we take action with what we know to create new value. Understanding this difference exposes one of the greatest problems facing school management and teaching: While we are good at managing information, we simply cannot manage the knowledge in students' heads without degrading it back to information.

9. **"The network is the learning"** (Siemens, 2007). The emerging pedagogy of this century isn't carefully planned. Rather, it's developed fluidly. Our traversals across networks are our pathways to learning, and as the network expands, so does our learning. In connectivist approaches to learning, we connect our individual knowledges together to create new understandings. We share our experiences and create new (social) knowledge as a result. We must center on the ability of individuals to navigate this space and make connections on their own, discovering how their unique knowledge and talents can be contextualized to solve new problems.

10. **The future belongs to nerds, geeks, makers, dreamers, and knowmads.** While not everybody will or should become an entrepreneur, those who do not develop entrepreneurial skills are at a great disadvantage. Our education systems should focus on the development of *entreprenerds*: individuals who leverage their specialized knowledge to dream, create, make, explore, learn and promote entrepreneurial, cultural, or social endeavors, taking risks and enjoying the process as much as the final outcome, without fearing the potential failures or mistakes that the journey includes.

11. **Break the rules, but understand *why*, clearly, first.** Our school systems are built on cultures of obedience, enforced compliance, and complacency. The creativities of students, staff, and our institutions are inherently stultified. It is easier to be told what to think than to think ourselves. Openly asking questions, and building a metacognitive awareness of what we have created and what we would like to do about it, can best cure this institutionalized malaise. Only then can we engineer justified breaks from the system that challenge the status quo and have the potential to create real impact.

12. **We *must* and *can* build cultures of trust in our schools and communities.** As long as our education systems continue to be based on fear, anxiety, and distrust, challenges to all of the above will continue. In the *Minnevate!* project (MASA, 2014), the researchers found that if educators are to build a collective capacity to transform education, we need engaged communities, and we also need to *engage with* the communities we serve. This requires a new theory of action, *centered on trust*, where students, schools, governments, businesses, parents, and communities may engage in collaborative initiatives to co-create new education futures.

Some say these principles require a revolution to be realized. Others say we need massive innovation to make positive education futures a reality. We believe we need both, or as Ronald van den Hoff (2013) says: "What we really need is an *innovution!*" (p. 236). And, this is our noble quest: To *innovute* with not only our ideas, but also the purposive applications of what we have learned through our individual efforts, and together, globally.

Initial signatories

We are: **John Moravec, PhD**, Education Futures (principal author, USA); **Daniel Araya, PhD**, University of Illinois at Urbana-Champaign (USA); **Daniel Cabrera, MD**, Mayo Clinic (USA); **Alexandra Castro**, Westhill Institute (Mexico); **Cristóbal Cobo, PhD**, Fundación Ceibal (Uruguay); **Guido Crolla**, HAN University of Applied Sciences (Netherlands); **Chloe Duff**, European Democratic Education Community (UK); **Maaike Eggermont**, Sudbury School Ghent (Belgium); **Martine Eyzenga**, Diezijnvaardig (Netherlands); **José García Contto**, Universidad de Lima (Peru); **Kristin Gehrmann**, Demokratische Schule München (Germany); **Peter Gray, PhD**, Boston College (USA); **Renske de Groot**, arts educator (Netherlands); **Leif Gustavson, PhD**, Pacific University (USA); **Peter Hartkamp**, The Quantum Company (Netherlands); **Christel Hartkamp-Bakker, PhD**, Newschool.nu (Netherlands); **Pekka Ihanainen**, Haaga-Helia School of Vocational Teacher Education (Finland); **Aaron Keohane**, Summerhill School (UK); **Nicola Kriesel**, BFAS e.V. (Germany); **Beatriz Miranda**, Aprendamos (Ecuador); **Sugata Mitra, PhD**, Newcastle University (UK); **Hugo Pardo Kuklinski, PhD**, Outliers School (Spain); **Tomis Parker**, Agile Learning Centers (USA); **Angela Peñaherrera**, Fraschini&Heller (Ecuador); **Robert Rogers, MD**, University of Maryland (USA); **Carlos Scolari, PhD**, Universitat Pompeu Fabra (Spain); **António Teixeira, PhD**, Universidade Aberta (Portugal); **Stephanie Thompson**, Beach Haven Primary (New Zealand); **Max Ugaz**, Economía Digital SAC (Peru); **Evert-Jan Ulrich**, Dutch Innovation School (Netherlands); **Charles Warcup**, Sudbury-Schule Ammersee (Germany); **Monika Wernz**, Sudbury-Schule Ammersee (Germany); **Alex Wiedermann**, Sudbury-Schule Ammersee (Germany)

REFERENCES

Cobo, C., & Moravec, J.W. (2011). *Aprendizaje Invisible: Hacia una nueva ecología de la educación.* Barcelona: Laboratori de Mitjans Interactius / Publicacions i Edicions de la Universitat de Barcelona. www.aprendizajeinvisible.com

EUDEC. (2005). EUDEC guidance document. European Democratic Education Community. www.eudec.org/dance+Document#Article_1:20_ Definitions

Gladstone, B. (Producer). (1999, November 30). The science in science fiction [Radio broadcast episode]. In Talk of the Nation. Washington, DC: National Public Radio. www.npr.org/templates/story/story.php?storyId=1067220

Gray, P. (2013). *Free to learn.* New York: Basic Books.

van den Hoff, R. (2013). Society30: Knowmads and new value creation. In J. W. Moravec (Ed.), *Knowmad Society* (pp. 231–252). Minneapolis: Education Futures.

MASA. (2014). Minnevate! 2013-2014 activity report. St. Paul, MN: Minnesota Association of School Administrators.

Moravec, J.W. (Ed.) (2013). *Knowmad Society.* Minneapolis: Education Futures.

Siemens, G. (2007). The network is the learning. www.youtube.com/watch?v=rpbkdeyFxZw

COLOPHON

**Emerging education futures:
Experiences and visions from the field**

Edited by John W. Moravec

Chapters authored by:
Leona Ungerer; Lisa B. Bosman, Julius C. Keller, & Gary R. Bertoline; Audrey Falk & Russell Olwell; Silvia Cecilia Enríquez, Sandra Beatriz Gargiulo, María Jimena Ponz & Erica Elena Scorians; Robert Thorn; Erling N. Dahl, Einar N. Strømmen & Tor G. Syvertsen; John W. Moravec & Kelly E. Killorn; Pekka Ihanainen; Stefania Saava; Gabriela Carreño Murillo; Erik Miletić

Illustration on pp. 140-141 by Zoe Moravec

Book design by Martine Eyzenga diezijnvaardig.nl

Cover photo adapted from original photo by Thomas Stephan on Unsplash.com

How to cite this book:
Moravec, J. W. (Ed.). (2019). *Emerging education futures: Experiences and visions from the field*. Minneapolis: Education Futures.

Published by Education Futures LLC
Minneapolis, Minnesota
educationfutures.com

Library of Congress Control Number: 2019915373

ISBN: 978-0-578-58059-3

Copyright © 2019 Education Futures LLC

This work is licensed under a Creative Commons Attribution-ShareAlike 4.0 International License. This means that you are free to use, redistribute, and create derivative works from this book as long as you give proper attribution to the authors, do not restrict access to your derivative work in any way, and license any derivative work you create from this book under an identical license. creativecommons.org/licenses/by-sa/4.0/

www.ingramcontent.com/pod-product-compliance
Lightning Source LLC
Chambersburg PA
CBHW072119270326
41931CB00010B/1605